Arthur,

Great to mee.

THE
AGE
OF
IDEAS

UNLOCK YOUR
CREATIVE POTENTIAL

ALAN PHILIPS

For requests, email alan@theageofideas.com

The Age of Ideas™ – Victor & Spoils Inc.

ISBN: 9781939126368

Printed in the United States of America.

Published by Zola Books
Zola Books, Inc.
143 West 29th Street
New York, NY 10001
Info@zolabooks.com

Visit Us
at
THEAGEOFIDEAS.COM

Cover & Logo Design by Magpie Studio, London
Book Design by Curtis Bohner
Copyedit by Phil Hanrahan

To my wife Gelareh, my partner on this journey of creation, you opened me up to believe in and connect with something greater. Thank you, I love you and I am in awe of your creativity and determination, always and forever I will be by your side.

To my sons River & Teddy, for proving that without a doubt there is something greater and its power is unimaginable. When I look at you I feel the most pure love I have ever known. You are my miracles. Never stop smiling and being true to yourself.

You are my life. Everything is for you.

Special Thanks:
Joe Regal & Family
Ben Christie & Magpie Studio
Harrison Boyce
Rodrigo Ortiz
Melody Godfred
Michael Bonadies
Carla Burt, Kirsten Magen, & The Hue & Cry Team

And all the friends, family, co-workers, and strangers who said yes, go on, don't stop and took those late night calls even when they didn't want to. Thank you for believing.

Table of Contents

PART FOUR: THE RULES OF MAGIC

CONCLUSION

APPENDIX

All human beings are born with the same creative potential. Most people squander theirs away on a million superfluous things. I expend mine on one thing and one thing only—my art.

—Pablo Picasso

PROLOGUE

The Traitorous Eight and the Start of Something Big

These were, by their résumés, very superior people. And I thought, gee, maybe there is something here, something more valuable than just being an employee.

—Arthur Rock, venture capitalist

On a hot summer morning in San Francisco in 1957, eight of the most talented young scientists in America convened for a clandestine meeting at the Clift Hotel. They gathered over breakfast in the famed Redwood Room, a bastion of the city's old guard. A nervous energy consumed the table, fueled by uncertainty, possibility, and fresh-brewed coffee. The eight worked on developing silicon semiconductors—a groundbreaking new technology—at Shockley Semiconductor outside of Palo Alto. The company's founder, Nobel Prize–winning scientist William Shockley, was a brilliant but difficult manager: erratic, mistrustful, and impatient. He had even gone so far as to hire detectives to give his employees lie-detector tests, and these employees, experts in a field in which there were few, were frustrated and angry.

After considering numerous options, the men decided they must defect. They planned to establish their own company under the leadership of MIT graduate Robert Noyce, a charming, personable twenty-nine-year-old electrical engineer from smalltown Iowa. Getting Noyce on board hadn't been easy. He was the leader they needed, but he had a young family, and he needed to be persuaded to leave his guaranteed paycheck for something with no model—creating a new company in a new field based on nothing more than combined knowledge, faith, ideas, and passion.

As Tom Wolfe would later write in *Esquire*:

"In this business, it dawned on them, capital assets in the traditional sense of plant, equipment, and raw materials counted for next to nothing. The only plant you needed was a shed big enough for the worktables. The only equipment you needed was some kilns, goggles, microscopes, tweezers, and diamond cutters. The materials, silicon and germanium, came from dirt and coal. Brainpower was the entire franchise."

Brainpower was the entire franchise.

After the meeting, the group's first move was to approach Shockley's main investor, Arnold Beckman. Beckman had been arguing with Shockley for months about spiraling research costs. Shockley had threatened to take his team elsewhere and find new money. But the eight scientists knew this was a bluff, and informed Beckman of their plan to leave. Despite a trio of positive meetings, Beckman ultimately said he was planning to stick with the senior researcher.

Fortunately for the employees, they had also contacted other possible investors, including thirty-year-old New York financier Arthur Rock, recipient of a letter they'd written explaining their situation. Their letter intrigued Rock, who was impressed with their backgrounds and experience, and Rock told them he wanted to go out and raise the money necessary for them to start their own company. The scientists agreed, and Rock began by sitting down with a copy of the *Wall Street Journal*, using it to compile a list of the thirty-five largest American companies. During the next few months, Rock diligently reached out to every one of them, and one by one they all said no. Disheartened, ready to move on, Rock received one last lead. An associate suggested he meet with Sherman Fairchild, a colorful, prominent entrepreneur and investor known for unconventional thinking. Founder of Fairchild Camera and Instrument, the son of IBM's first chairman, Fairchild immediately recognized a potent opportunity and backed the men to the tune of $1.5 million.

On that June 1957 morning, the eight men didn't have an official contract, so instead they all signed a crisp dollar bill. One by one, these technology pioneers—Robert Noyce, Julius Blank, Victor Grinich, Jean Hoerni, Eugene Kleiner, Jay Last, Gordon Moore, and

Sheldon Roberts—added a signature to their own declaration of independence, framing what would be a history-making choice: they would pursue their visionary ideas inside the structure of a new, innovative company.

With the financial backing of Fairchild, the eight men founded Fairchild Semiconductor in a location just twelve blocks from Shockley's facility. Long before the term "Silicon Valley startup" existed, this trailblazing operation in Mountain View, California, helped produce technology destined to change the world, and incubated extraordinary talent.

Two of the "traitorous eight," as Shockley called them—Noyce and Moore—would eventually leave to found Intel Corporation. Austrian-born industrial engineer Eugene Kleiner invested in Intel before starting the legendary venture capital firm Kleiner-Perkins in 1972, a firm that would one day fund Amazon, Google, AOL, Compaq, Genentech, and many others. As for Arthur Rock, he unknowingly gave birth to the multi-billion-dollar industry of tech-based venture capital. In time Rock himself would lead the investment in Apple. To complete our circle, Apple founder Steve Jobs would consider Robert Noyce a mentor, and even, some would say, a surrogate father. Taken together, the original employees of Fairchild Semiconductor can be said to have created or helped create hundreds of new companies and technologies.

A revolution of consciousness and creative capital had begun.

PART ONE: THE POWER OF IDEAS

A Night in Little Italy

My story begins in January 2008. I'd just returned from Christmas vacation and was in good spirits. The hospitality marketing company I'd been running since college had completed its best year ever. We'd doubled revenues for a third consecutive year. My partners and I were so encouraged that we decided to expand our office, invest in new computers and phone systems, and hire new employees, including my older brother, who was tasked with creating a new sponsorship marketing division. Things were looking good.

And then it all fell apart.

Mere months after our expansion, the global financial system imploded. We went from having more than a dozen high-profile clients paying tens of thousands of dollars in monthly retainers to zero in roughly a week. Nothing quite prepares you for an experience like that. It immediately resets your priorities and puts you face to face with your biggest fears as an entrepreneur—failure and letting down the people who count on you.

We went into survival mode. We had enough cash on hand to carry us through maybe two months, but we needed to figure out a way to cut costs and get some revenue coming in. Time was not on our side. We scrapped, fought, landed a client or two, moved into an office share, cut unnecessary expenses, and survived. And though shared struggle often creates stronger bonds, in this case that didn't happen. The world had changed, the business had changed, and so had I.

The crash—and my failure—woke me from a self-indulgent slumber and forced me to take a hard look at what I had been doing and why. When I started in the hospitality business, it had been because of my passion for food and for watching people enjoy the experiences we created. Since boyhood, to me a good meal meant a connection to all my favorite things in the world—it was love. This passion had led me, at age sixteen, to score a coveted culinary stage in Wolfgang Puck's kitchen at the original Spago on Sunset Boulevard. From there, it took me to Cornell's Hotel School and got me in the door for some great hospitality and business training.

But somewhere along the way I'd gotten off track. I had been seduced by the energy and ego of the entertainment world. I became more interested in short-term material success and getting my name in the newspaper than in building something that was high quality and had deeper meaning. Something that would last. Something of substance. While my approach had worked for a while, my financial success really was just an enabler, allowing me to avoid seeing the real issues with the business and with myself.

That challenging experience in 2008 proved pivotal. Early the next year, I made decisions that redirected my path. As 2009 began, it was clear my company was no longer where my passion resided. After much soul-searching, I came to the realization that I needed to get back to what I loved most—food and hospitality.

But it wasn't until a late night out in New York City when an unexpected encounter unlocked a new, creative direction in my life. My cousin Rob and I hit a bar in Little Italy and afterward decided to get some pasta. The only problem? It was after two in the morning. We went to the one place we could find open, and over plates of spaghetti and meatballs we struck up a conversation with the establishment's owner. I'll call him Gino. Gino told us he was losing money and needed a way to generate more revenue. His restaurant had expanded aggressively from its original location in the building's basement. At three times the size and staff, the costs were too much for him to handle. Gino told us the original space—once a famous hangout for Frank Sinatra and the Rat Pack—remained in vintage condition, serving now as a private party space with its own entrance.

Gino gave us a tour of the former Sinatra haunt, and as he did, a realization hit. If I wanted to get back to my roots in the restaurant business, the best way to do it—the best way to prove what I was capable of—would be to create a pop-up, a temporary restaurant. And here was an amazing space with a legendary past known to almost no one in one of the world's great restaurant cities. I had to give it a shot.

The stars seemed to be aligned, because everything came together perfectly. Reservations for the multiday run sold out in under twenty-four hours. Our concept was not only a financial success, it was covered by local, national, and international media outlets, with a feature in *W* magazine, a segment on The Cooking Channel, and articles in the *New York Post*, the *New York Times*, and *Crain's*, among others. Reality-TV producers descended, but we avoided them like the plague. The opening night, celebrity chef Tom Colicchio of *Top Chef* was there, along with a who's who of the New York food world. But more rewarding than the prominent clientele was the fact that everyone enjoyed themselves—the room's mood was warm, beautiful, fun. And those present loved the idea that they were enjoying a one-of-a-kind dining experience, shared with a cozy number of fellow food-lovers.

It was a memorable night for a burgeoning community of food enthusiasts at exactly the right moment. I was ecstatic. For the first time in my adult life, I was doing something purely for the joy of sharing my passion with the world, rather than to stroke my ego or make money. It felt like I was finally living my purpose. I was manifesting my dreams, making tangible an inspiration that came from deep within.

I followed that first pop-up with many more. My team and I launched a temporary art installation-restaurant in a hotel construction site in midtown Manhattan; a Roaring Twenties steakhouse with the amazing chef Seamus Mullen (with whom I would later open a restaurant in London); a downtown version of New York's famous Le Cirque; and a short-run satellite of Cantinetta Antinori, a Tuscan restaurant run by the Antinori wine family, the oldest family-run business in the world.

Since then I've continued to produce curated dining and hospitality experiences, most recently with Dinner Party, a multicity dining experience in partnership with Vice Media. Dinner Party has featured food from chefs such as Andy Ricker of Pok Pok, Carlo Mirarchi of Roberta's, and Stuart Brioza and Nicole Krasinski of State Bird Provisions. These pop-up enterprises connect with guests because they bring together people—both employees and customers—who care deeply about the project, and share a special experience.

Creating the pop-ups—doing something that was a pure reflection of my passions—changed my life. The core idea and drive to execute what I envisioned enabled me to realize my potential for the first time. That shift in how I approached the world supercharged all other areas of my existence. I went from being a struggling entrepreneur to heading up a food and beverage business with $150 million in annual revenue to chief marketing officer of a publicly-traded hotel company to head of brand and experience at a billion-dollar startup in less than five years. And not only did the pop-up restaurant experience provide me with the opportunity to share my creativity on a large scale while supporting my family, it also gave me the gift of fulfillment and the confidence to trust my instincts and enjoy the journey as much as, if not more than, the result.

All of that flowed from manifesting an idea that aligned with my purpose. By "manifesting," I simply mean making the intangible tangible. Making a dream reality. Executing on a vision. It changed my life, this idea, but if you think about it, a pop-up restaurant is really just a catering event repackaged with creativity and purpose. However, because we live in a time when purpose-driven ideas have more power than ever before, the concept transcended its components.

My goal in this book to show you how this all works. I want to give you the confidence and knowledge to unleash your superpower—your own creative potential.

THE AGE OF IDEAS

A point in time when creativity becomes the primary driver of value creation and the last remaining sustainable competitive advantage.

And Then One Day Everything Changed...

It is as if Freud supplied us the sick half of psychology, and we must now fill it out with the healthy half.

—Abraham Maslow

It's fitting that Abraham Maslow, the man behind the concept of the hierarchy of needs, was born in Brooklyn, the city that has come to define the twenty-first-century brand for living a creative existence. Born in 1908 to immigrant Russian parents, Maslow was raised in a very different Brooklyn. His early years were marked by poverty, anti-Semitism, a toxic relationship with his parents, and a lack of self-confidence, but through a combination of extraordinary intelligence—he was reputed to have an IQ of 195—hard work, and the stability of a happy marriage, Maslow persevered and developed theories that expanded our understanding of the human experience.

Prior to Maslow's breakthroughs, psychology had focused on what was wrong with people—their neuroses, their mental illnesses. But after witnessing the atrocities of World War II, Maslow theorized that this conventional approach was limited. He created humanistic psychology—the study of unlocking human potential.

Maslow's work changed the course of psychology by concentrating on how people could flourish by amplifying what was right about them rather than trying to modify and correct their psychic weaknesses. This cornerstone belief was reflected in his approach to therapy. He looked at people seeking help as clients instead of patients, and strove to establish warm human dynamics with them, not clinical, impersonal physician/patient relationships. With this emotional connection as a basis for action, Maslow then set about working with these clients to improve their lives.

He believed every human has a powerful desire to realize his or her full potential. Maslow's term for reaching that goal was self-actualization, which he understood as "expressing one's creativity, quest for spiritual enlightenment, pursuit of knowledge, and the desire to give to society" within daily life. If an individual is able to self-actualize, they become capable of having "peak experiences," which he defined as "rare, exciting, oceanic, deeply moving, exhilarating, elevating experiences that generate an advanced form of perceiving reality, and are even mystic and magical in their effect upon the experimenter."

Sounds pretty spectacular, right?

But Maslow also stated that the basic needs of humans must be met before a person can achieve self-actualization and enjoy peak experiences. That means unless you have adequate food, shelter, warmth, security, and a sense of belonging, you're unable to reach this higher consciousness. Not until the twentieth century had any significant portion of humanity had their basic needs met for a sustained period.

The Assembly Line

The year 1908 not only featured the birth of a man who would take psychology in a new direction, but it was also a revolutionary year for organizations, including the Ford Motor Company. 1908 was when Ford introduced the Model T, the first widely available and affordable consumer automobile. For years, Henry Ford had been maniacally focused on his goal of producing a simple, reliable car that would be financially accessible to the average American worker. But in order to build his dream, Ford realized he needed to eliminate the handcrafted construction process and replace it with a more automated system to expedite production.

The idea for the system Ford needed was introduced to him when an associate visited slaughterhouses in Chicago. These slaughterhouses disassembled animal carcasses as they moved along a conveyor belt. Ford realized he could use this process in reverse, approaching the construction of the automobile as an assembly line, using standardized parts and unskilled labor. This allowed him to radically increase his production capabilities and significantly decrease his costs.

While Ford didn't invent the concept, he perfected it. Prior to the assembly line's arrival, it took twelve and a half hours to build a Model T—a slow, expensive process performed by teams of skilled workmen in multiple locations. The assembly line flipped the process on its head. Instead of the workers going to the car, the car came to the workers, and they could perform one part of the process over and over. Ford was able to reduce the time it took to build a Model T to just ninety-three minutes, allowing him to produce eight times the number of cars in the same time-frame.

The impact of the assembly line wasn't only felt at Ford—it became a key development in growing the world economy across the twentieth century. Manufacturers were now capable of producing significantly more volume at much lower costs. And with the introduction of unions, workers were paid higher wages for their efforts, creating the consumer base necessary to purchase all the products that were being generated.

While the assembly line created some meaningful advances in society, it widened the gap between the haves and the have-nots by solidifying a tremendous barrier to entry for manufacturing businesses. Factories and assembly lines cost millions and millions of dollars to build, and those resources were only available to large organizations and wealthy industrialists. That made it nearly impossible to disrupt or innovate without being associated with one of these entities.

The assembly line also marked a tipping point for standardization and globalization. Prior to its arrival there was a strong emotional connection between the artisan and the product. The maker was close to the consumer, and that meant something to both of them. Standardized production over the twentieth century eroded that connection by separating the producer from the product. Producers no longer had to be skilled—they now only had to handle a piece of the process. That, with very few exceptions, systematically eliminated specialized artisan work. And the more efficient production became, the more financially beneficial it was to consolidate on the retail side as well, which led to what most call globalization, but I call global monotony. We entered the "Boring Age," one in which different cities and countries all featured the same stores and products.

The best example of this phenomenon took place in the fashion industry. Louis Vuitton, Gucci, Christian Dior, Chanel, Tiffany—these were all individual artisans or shopkeepers, people or families who worked hard at their craft and established a strong business by building a reputation for quality and a direct connection with their customers. During the past century, a majority of these businesses were acquired by conglomerates that centralized production in large factories in third-world countries. The conglomerates then rapidly expanded the retail operations to satisfy growth targets, allowing a product that had once only been available in select markets to be available almost anywhere. Eventually, a name that stood so clearly for handcrafted, one-of-a-kind products became just another shop among a sea of sameness. The experience of traveling to a far-flung location to experience something special or different was gone. Instead, the consumer would just wait for the inevitable sale at their local retail mall to purchase the once unforgettable items for fifty percent off.

The Shift

> *For every action, there is an equal and opposite reaction.*
>
> —Isaac Newton

And then one day everything changed; the world shifted on its axis, our consciousness evolved. Instead of making their purchase decisions based solely on price, people became willing to pay more for sustainable or organic products. They no longer wanted their meat mass-produced; they wanted grass-fed beef from a local farmer. Rather than just a good sweat from their exercise, they also wanted mindfulness, so they took up SoulCycle, yoga, or meditation. And rather than settling down to buy their dream home and build their 401k, they spent their resources searching out experiences they could share and cherish more than they would another purse or car. Above all else, they wouldn't accept the status quo. Instead of working in secure yet unfulfilling jobs, they wanted to create an existence that reflected their innermost desires and beliefs. And they did, in record numbers.

Millennials and The Millennial Mindset

Let's return to Abraham Maslow. Remember, he asserted that the basic needs of humans—food, shelter, warmth, security, and sense of belonging—must be met before they can achieve self-actualization. And today, for the first time in human history, a large portion of the population is no longer consumed by daily concern for their basic needs.

In one of his recent letters to shareholders, Warren Buffett addressed this:

"Most of today's children are doing well. All families in my upper middle-class neighborhood regularly enjoy a living standard better than that achieved by John D. Rockefeller Sr. at the time of my birth. His unparalleled fortune couldn't buy what we now take for granted, whether the field is—to name just a few—transportation, entertainment, communication or medical services. Rockefeller certainly had power and fame; he could not, however, live as well as my neighbors now do."

Freed from incessant worry about securing the bare essentials to live, the majority of us in the Western world are able to focus on tending to our higher needs—on pursuing happiness, on thriving. And one group has benefited from this shift more than all the rest—millennials, the largest, most diverse generation ever.

Millennials, those Americans born between 1980 and the early 2000s, spent their youth in relatively comfortable surroundings. They watched as their parents—the Baby Boomers and Gen Xers—obeyed the rules of the industrial complex, getting steady corporate jobs and saving for retirement. Their parents achieved modern society's definition of success: material wealth. But millennials could see that, rather than bringing fulfillment, this path often ended with their parents unhappy, divorced, stressed-out, or on antidepressants. In response to this, millennials went in another direction. Well-educated and communicative, they learned from their parents' experiences and adjusted their needs hierarchy to put meaning ahead of money.

Millennials want lives marked by creativity, spiritual satisfaction, expanded knowledge, societal contribution, and multilayered experiences. Sound familiar? We're in Maslow territory—millennials are seeking to live self-actualized lives and enjoy peak experiences, a generational change that has had extensive repercussions.

The Platform Business Model

As we saw, Henry Ford changed the world by combining his vision for a mass-produced, affordable automobile with the concept of an assembly line. The problem was that the barrier to entry to any industry was so great that only the rich or existing corporations could play, so his system gave the majority of the power and money to the few rather than the many. But over the last thirty or so years, some very smart people in Silicon Valley changed the world yet again. With the Internet and mobility becoming widely available, they created a new way of communicating and doing business centered around platforms.

A platform is a raised, level surface on which people or things can stand. A platform business works in just that way: it allows users—producers and consumers of goods, services, and content—to create, communicate, and consume value through the platform. Amazon, Apple's App Store, eBay, Airbnb, Facebook, LinkedIn, PayPal, YouTube, Uber, Wikipedia, Instagram, etsy, Twitter, Snapchat, Hotel Tonight, Salesforce, Kickstarter, and Alibaba are all platform businesses. While these businesses have done many impressive things, the most relevant to us is that they have created an opportunity for anyone, even those with limited means, to share their thoughts, ideas, creativity, and creations with millions of people at a low cost.

Today, if you create a product or have an idea, you can sell that product or share that idea with a substantial audience quickly and cost-effectively through these platforms. Not only that, but the platforms arguably give more power to individuals than corporations since they're so efficient at identifying ulterior motives or lack of authenticity. The communities on these platforms, many of whom are millennials, know when they're being sold to rather than shared with, and quickly eliminate those users from their consciousness (a/k/a their social media feeds).

Now, smaller organizations and less prosperous individuals are able to sell to or share their products, services, or content with more targeted demographics of people. That's exactly what the modern consumer desires: a more personalized, connected experience. For example, a Brooklyn handbag designer can sell her handbags to a select group of customers through one of the multitude of fashion or shopping platforms and create an ongoing dialogue with her audience through a communication platform such as Instagram. Or an independent filmmaker from Los Angeles can create a short film using a GoPro and the editing software on their Mac and then instantly share it with countless people through one of a dozen video platforms and get direct feedback. Or an author can write a book and sell it directly from his or her website and social channels to anyone who's excited about it. The reaction to standardization and globalization has been enabled by these platforms. Customers can get what they want, from whomever they want, whenever they want it. It's a revised and personalized version of globalization that allows us to maintain and enhance the cultural connections that create the meaning we crave in our lives.

The Result

Now that the barrier to entry has been significantly diminished—no more big factories and assembly lines—ideas, intangibles, and creativity have more value and influence than ever before. This changes what's possible for the majority of humanity. A talented teenager starts designing clothes in school, creates a following on Instagram, and a few months later ends up doing a capsule collection for Nike, the biggest sneaker company in the world. A singer shares her renditions of covers on YouTube, is contacted by A&R from a record label, and a couple of years later becomes the hottest thing in the music business. Or an engineer shares his idea and business plan on Kickstarter and is fully funded and on the road to building his dream in just twenty-four hours.

Extraordinary opportunity is now available and accessible to individuals and organizations with the creativity, passion, ambition, and work ethic to manifest their ideas. And, coincidentally, this is happening at the exact same time that a growing portion of the population is seeking out and rewarding creators for their work. Millennials (and those living with a millennial mind-set) support and consume products, services, and content made by passionate and authentic individuals and organizations they feel a connection with. That's what we call a product-market fit. Except it isn't a micro-market—it's the largest market in the world, and that has changed everything.

Welcome to the Age of Ideas.

That's Great, But How Does This Apply To Me?

You have been born into a time when anything is possible and all the tools to make your dreams real are available and, for the most part, affordable. Your ancestors fought to remove the restraints of monarchy and dictatorship, your parents and grandparents were the guinea pigs who struggled with the limitations of the industrial system, and you are the beneficiary of it all. You now have the freedom to pursue your own path, discover your best self, and connect with a community that helps you proceed along this journey. There is nothing holding you back.

If you don't have the necessary education, go watch some videos on YouTube and start learning.

If you don't have an audience, start a social media account and begin building relationships.

If you don't have the money to pursue your project, put together a pitch-deck and start raising it. Or better yet, bootstrap your project and work on it in the evenings after you finish your day job.

The game didn't just change—the field got turned upside down and inside out. And most people don't understand how the new paradigm works, giving those that do an even greater advantage. Your ideas have more power than ever before, and when you understand how to manifest and share those ideas, you can make a substantial impact.

Unlocking that value inside of you is what this book is all about.

I am guided by the belief that everyone desires freedom, fulfillment, and success. All three come from understanding the emotional elements and transforming them into sharable creative expressions. This gives your life and business meaning.

In the modern market, meaning is what generates value, making your creativity the primary driver of future value creation and the last remaining sustainable competitive advantage.

Everything you could ever want or need to start a business and share your ideas is just a click away. You want to start a coffee company? Partner with a local roaster, brand your beans, and go. From Starbucks to Blue Bottle to the local coffee shop around the corner, the coffee you are drinking is a highly accessible commodity. When you pay a premium for a branded cup, you are paying for the creativity that went into that cup. The store design, creativity; the cup design, creativity; the marketing, creativity; the experience, creativity. The Unicorn Frappuccino is not a miracle of mother nature, it's a miracle of human creativity and marketing. Everything that makes a cup of Starbucks coffee worth five dollars is somehow tied to the creativity and beliefs of the Starbucks organization.

Bottled water is another example. Free, high-quality water is available in much of the developed world. But the developed world is exactly where the majority of bottled water is consumed. In 2012, in the U.S. alone, we spent $11.8 billion dollars on bottled water. Because packaging is a fixed price and water is a low-priced commodity, what exactly are we paying the rest of the money for? The answer is that much of the value is tied up in the brand, the idea, how it makes you feel, the creativity.

The point I'm making is that in the Age of Ideas the barrier to entry exists more in our minds than it does in the real world. Differentiation and value today come from unlocking your creative potential, not owning a factory or a farm. The only sustainable competitive advantage left is being the best version of yourself. Manifesting your creativity via sharable forms such as products, services, or entertainment—that produces your advantage. The meaning behind your passion, whether it be for hospitality, law, or hot sauce, now translates into value. In the Age of Ideas this is what the market demands, and you have the power to give it to them by unlocking your unique creative potential.

Ian Schrager

Making the spirit soar and making somebody sort of lift off the ground and fly is about creating magic. People ask me about magic and what it is; it's very difficult for me to say. If I knew I would write a book and sell the book. And that magic, that very elusive kind of thing, is what I try to create at these hotels.

—Ian Schrager

As we pulled up to the porte cochère, I remember being thrilled. The entrance to the Delano had a magnitude and energy I'd rarely, if ever, experienced before. The valets were all perfectly dressed in crisp white outfits, the people getting out of their cars were beautifully put together, and the architecture was the perfect combination of classic Art Deco and clean modern lines.

While the arrival alone was magnificent, it wasn't until I entered the lobby that I was swept away: fifty-foot ceilings, a straight-shot visual hundreds of feet from the entrance to the rear orchard, and charming vignettes of whimsical seating and social areas throughout. The beauty was unmistakable, and the energy was so real you could almost drink it. Every step I took built on the drama of the experience. By the time I exited the lobby and stepped into the orchard, I felt changed, as if my appreciation for what the imagination could manifest had been heightened. I didn't say a word for ten minutes after I walked outside. I just smiled, completely satisfied by what I had just consumed.

While the experience was powerful, as in many meaningful moments, I wasn't fully aware of how this night would affect me. I definitely wasn't aware I would end up spending over a decade of my life involved in different ways with this company, crafting new ideas, creating even more magical experiences. What I did know, without a doubt, was that I had tasted fully realized creative potential. And once I knew it existed, how could I live without realizing my own? So I began my research at the source: Ian Schrager, the iconoclastic creator of Delano.

Schrager, like Maslow, was born in Brooklyn to a working-class family. Unlike Maslow, he had a close relationship with his parents, especially with his father, Louis, who instilled in him a strong value system. After spending his youth in East Flatbush, he headed off to Syracuse University in 1964. That's where he met Steve Rubell, another Brooklyn product, who would become his lifelong friend and business partner. An outgoing, flamboyant character, Steve was a couple of years older than Ian, but the two meshed perfectly. As Ian tells it, "We were dating the same girl, and from the way we went about competing for her, we came to respect and like each other. And the friendship just got closer and closer and closer. I would say that from the end of 1964 until Steve died in 1989 I spoke to him every single day."

After they graduated, Ian went on to practice real estate law, and Steve started a chain of steakhouses and became Ian's first client. It was about this time that Ian and Steve started going to clubs together, and they were astonished and inspired by what they saw. For the first time they were exposed to the mixing of different groups of people, the breaking down of social barriers—and the willingness of people to stand in line for the chance to spend their money. This was when Ian began to sense his desire to create. After a couple of months of going out and throwing a few parties of their own, Ian and Steve decided to open their own disco—in Queens, a borough of New York City known more for slicked-back hair and slice shops than for chic parties and celebrities.

After their first club, Enchanted Garden, was a financial success, Ian and Steve soon wanted to take the next big step: a club in Manhattan. By early 1977, they'd signed the lease for a former CBS studio and opera house on West Fifty-Fourth Street. It took them six weeks and $400,000 to transform the old theater into a nightclub. They kept much of the original infrastructure and used it to rig lighting that would constantly change the feel and create the energy needed to make the club a transformative experience.

As Schrager once put it, "With a nightclub, you have no real discernible product. You have the same music and the same alcohol as everybody else, and yet you have to create magic night after night in hopes of distinguishing yourself." On April 26, 1977, Studio 54 opened, and the world of nightlife would never be the same.

For the thirty-three months that followed, Studio 54 was the center of the universe. Ian, Steve, and their team would combine their unlimited imagination with hard work and execution to create that magic night after night. There were countless legendary moments: Bianca Jagger riding into the club on a white horse for her birthday celebration; a nineteen-year-old Michael Jackson on the dance floor with Andy Warhol, Liza Minelli, Steven Tyler, Brooke Shields, and the Village People; elaborate theme parties celebrating everyone from Karl Lagerfeld to Elizabeth Taylor. The regulars at 54 included Halston, Mick Jagger, Jerry Hall, Debbie Harry, Grace Jones, Calvin Klein, Elton John, Tina Turner, Divine, Margaret Trudeau, Francesco Scavullo, Truman Capote, Margaux Hemingway, Freddie Mercury, Tommy Hilfiger, Mikhail Baryshnikov, Diana Ross,

Al Pacino, Cher, Bruce Jenner, David Bowie, Iman, Salvador Dali, Diana Vreeland, John Travolta, Beverly Johnson, Lauren Hutton, Andre Leon Talley, Diane von Furstenberg, and Jacqueline Kennedy Onassis. Studio 54 was surreal. It became more than a place—it was a moment etched in time, capturing the energy of the sexual revolution in unbridled freedom and hedonism. Studio 54 was the apogee of escapism.

Ian and Steve weren't ready for the sudden explosion of energy and material success and let it inflate their egos. In December 1978, Steve was quoted in a newspaper saying that Studio 54 had made $7 million in its first year of operation and "only the Mafia made more money." Shortly thereafter, the nightclub was raided, and Steve and Ian were arrested for skimming $2.5 million without paying taxes. Charged with tax evasion, obstruction of justice, and conspiracy, they were sentenced to three and a half years in prison. In a blink of an eye, they had gone from the top of the world to the lowest place they could ever imagine.

After prison, Steve and Ian were motivated to regain what they'd lost. They opened another nightclub, Palladium, in Manhattan's historic Academy of Music building. Ian enlisted world-renowned Japanese architect Arata Isozaki to reimagine the space, and they made art the focal point of the experience, with installations by Jean-Michel Basquiat, Julian Schnabel, Kenny Scharf, Keith Haring, and Francesco Clemente. It was another legendary success. While Steve was passionate about recapturing the days of 54, Ian saw another club as repeating themselves. "If you repeat yourself," he stated, "there isn't any point. I'm always looking for something else—trying to pull a rabbit out of a hat." To him, Palladium was a stopover on the way to the duo's next big challenge: hotels.

With their nightclubs, Ian and Steve had to create something out of nothing. While people love nightclubs, there's no practical need a club fulfills. Going to one is an act of desire, a want, for escape or social validation—it's all emotional. On the other hand, people need hotels; they need a place to stay, so there's a practical value. Now, instead of pulling a rabbit out of the nightclub hat every night, Ian and Steve had to figure out how to reinvent the hotel experience by adding emotional elements. "Hotels," Ian once said, "are in certain important ways, nightclubs for grown-ups....

So when Steve and I went into the hotel business, where we had a real commodity that people wanted, we didn't rely on that. Our approach wasn't, well, we have a bed. Our approach was, we want to make it something magical."

And they did. Ian and Steve knew there were no hotels catering to the taste and lifestyle of their clientele. It was obvious to them that the hotel business was stale with sameness; if they could infuse art and lifestyle into this segment of commerce, they would disrupt the industry.

Their first hotel, Morgans, opened in 1984, and it was a revelation. They'd hired a designer, Andrée Putman, who had never done a hotel before, and gave her the freedom to design the experience without any rules. Every detail was considered, from art in the rooms (one-of-a-kind photographs by Robert Mapplethorpe), to the most chic bars and restaurants and avant-garde public spaces. Steve described their new hotel by saying that if a Holiday Inn or a Marriott were like Macy's or Bloomingdale's, their new hotel was like a Madison Avenue boutique. And just like that, the boutique hotel was born.

Following the success of Morgans, Ian went on to open the Royalton and Paramount hotels, introducing the concept of "lobby socializing," which made the lobby a dynamic city social center, and "cheap chic"—the idea of affordable luxury in a stylish environment. Next, Schrager invented the "urban resort" with Delano Miami—ironically, the hotel his parents had brought him to on their first family vacation many years before. With each hotel, he changed the perspectives of guests and the hospitality industry on what was possible.

Since then, Ian has continued his groundbreaking, space-defining work with Mondrian Los Angeles, Hudson New York, Clift San Francisco, and St. Martins Lane and Sanderson in London. More recently, he launched his Edition hotel brand in partnership with Marriott, his own cheap-chic brand Public hotels, and a slew of residential real estate projects in downtown Manhattan. He has collaborated with some of the most creative designers, artists, and restaurateurs in the world, including Philippe Starck, Julian Schnabel, Herzog de Mueron, John Pawson, Yabu Pushelberg, Jean-Georges Vongerichten, and many more. *Travel & Leisure* magazine summed it up perfectly by saying, "Ian Schrager has done more to bring design to the travel experience than any other living person—single-handedly reinventing the hotel as a site of electrifying cultural significance."

While many say Schrager's work is about design, it isn't—it's about ideas and experiences. Ian uses the power of his ideas to tap into what he calls the "collective unconsciousness, the ethereal, elusive, and hard-to-define magic and energy." He understands the power of this intangible, emotional place and uses it to connect deeply with his customers. He knows that *"the way a product makes you feel is more important than how it looks. The goal is to create experiences that people will remember, to touch them in emotional and visceral ways, to lift their spirits, to assault their senses, and to wow them in tasteful ways."* But just as important, Schrager understands that an amazing experience can't be created from ideas alone, knowing that "good execution is just as important as a good idea." And he has consistently manifested his creative potential because he has regularly married the four key elements that create value in our new age: purpose, creativity, execution, and emotion.

Ian Schrager creates because he has to, not because he wants to. He isn't competing against anyone except himself. As he says: "It is never about the money—but instead to get people even more excited than they were the last time." And with a little help from his friend, that's how he unlocked his creative potential.

Shifting Perception

> *Brand is just a perception, and perception will match reality over time. Sometimes it will be ahead, other times it will be behind. But brand is simply a collective impression some have about a product.*
>
> —Elon Musk

Great ideas have the power to shift perception to create value where it didn't exist before. Remember when I mentioned earlier that when I created my pop-up restaurants, I was concerned people would realize they were just catering events, repackaged and marketed from a different perspective? Well, let's explore this phenomenon a little more.

GREAT IDEAS HAVE
THE POWER TO
SHIFT PERCEPTION
TO CREATE VALUE
WHERE IT DIDN'T
EXIST BEFORE.

For a number of years, I worked at Morgans Hotel Group, the company founded by Ian Schrager. As we just explored, Schrager gets credit for originating lifestyle, or boutique, hotels. Such hotels have a distinct design, unique story, and creatively programmed public spaces such as restaurants, pools, spas, and lobbies. But all full-service hotels have always been designed and made up of rooms and public spaces. What Schrager did when he developed the lifestyle hotel was apply his creativity—through design, story-telling, and programming—to shift the customer's perspective and produce significant value. After all, many lifestyle hotels are just underperforming hotel assets that have been repositioned using these creative elements.

After Morgans, I joined a leader in the coworking field. Coworking is an evolving idea and exploding industry, but at a basic level it can be defined as an enterprise that offers shared workplaces for people—freelancers, employees of startups, small and large companies—attracted to the community the space creates and by the coworking company's philosophy, story, and creativity. Instead of leasing buildings in a traditional manner to multiple larger tenants, coworking companies lease entire structures and then sell these leases at a higher rate to members, a/k/a tenants. A change in use, not physical form. Combine that with the intangibles of inventive branding and experiential activation, and you've transformed one of the largest industries in the world—commercial real estate—simply by changing the way people perceive it.

But does that kind of thing last? Is it sustainable? Well, let's look at the facts. In the years after my first pop-up, pop-ups became a global craze, right alongside food trucks. Pop-ups are being regularly produced by restaurant companies, magazines, culinary collectives, hotel groups, and stadiums. Additionally, the hospitality industry has taken the concepts of supper clubs, guest chefs, and theme dinners, and stitched them into the playbook guiding the operations of restaurants and other food and beverage operations. Conclusion: pop-ups are now part of the hospitality vernacular, serving multiple functions, from stand-alone profitable businesses to driving extra profits for existing restaurants to testing new concepts.

Next up, lifestyle hotels. Since the concept arrived in 1984, it has revolutionized the hotel and hospitality industry. After Ian

Schrager and Morgans, we saw W Hotels, Joie de Vivre, Kimpton, André Balaz, Viceroy, Ace, and dozens more brands and thousands of independent hotels. As of 2015, thirty years after their creation, lifestyle hotels represented over twenty percent of the total hotel industry. Every major hotel company now has one or more lifestyle-brand offerings. Not only that, but the segment has completely changed the way non-lifestyle hotels operate, forcing the hand of the incumbents to tell better stories about who they are, offer more interesting food, beverage, and public space experiences, and implement specific design perspectives that appeal to their target clientele. And the move toward a more lifestyle-centric approach to hospitality has bled into other industries like residential apartments, fitness, and even retail.

As for coworking, while the story is still being written, there are tens of billions of dollars being invested in the industry, multiple players in every major city in the world, and a movement of freelancers, entrepreneurs, and large companies looking for a better way to work. The complete integration of work and leisure is upon us, and coworking is one of the key solutions satisfying this cultural shift. Again, it principally offers a change in usage and a way to identify emotionally as part of a community, not a new technology or practical offering. This makes coworking a shift very much driven by branding, storytelling, and perception. Who knows how this story will end? But it seems like the way we work in the future will be changed by the effect coworking has had on the collective consciousness.

This same theory of shifting perception applies to individuals. For years, celebrities have had armies of people helping them craft very particular visions of who they are, which has generated tremendous value. For example, female teen stars are told to embrace a sexier image and take edgier roles as they get older, so their fans will begin to perceive them as adult actors and follow them as they move to the next level of their careers. Tom Cruise's team carefully crafted his image for decades, which made him wealthy and powerful. Then one day he decided to go off script on Oprah's show, jump on her couch, and make some controversial comments, which dented his carefully curated image, and cost him millions in future earnings. As the Huffington Post put it, "Though Cruise's name is still a big box-office draw, these days, he is better known for being an outspoken advocate for Scientology and for his public antics. The couch jump marked the first shift in Tom Cruise's image away from the heartthrob he'd been." Over time Cruise regained some of his lost cultural capital, but the impact was significant, and it's a vivid example of perception impacting value.

The thing is, in the Age of Ideas, *regular people are able to harness the power of perception in the same way celebrities and big companies have for years.* Whether on LinkedIn, Facebook, Instagram, or personal blogs, you can influence your value by affecting how people perceive you. And the same way an entrepreneur can change the value of a building or event by changing people's perception of it, you too can change people's perception of you through authentic storytelling.

It's critical we understand and learn from the above examples. We exist in a time that values creativity more than ever. By shifting the perception of a person, product, or place, you will significantly impact their value and how the market interacts with them. Perception is closer to reality than ever before, and your ability to positively shift perception directly correlates to how much value you can create in the Age of Ideas.

Creative Potential

Let's discuss creativity for a moment. Creativity is that special something. It can take you from good to great, from want to need, from admiration to infatuation. It is intangible, emotional, and premium-worthy. It's honest. It's simple. It's generous. It's beautiful to watch and effortless to enjoy. Once you get in touch with your creativity, nothing else is ever the same. It is an energy deep within, one that connects us all.

The way to create value in the Age of Ideas is to identify, manifest, and share your creativity.

A little far out for you? Let me elaborate.

If you've ever fallen in love—and I hope you have—you'd know that it is quite an unexplainable emotion. There's no questioning it when it happens. When you feel love, it's unmistakably present, and when you don't, there's no doubting its absence.

**THE WAY TO
CREATE VALUE IN
THE AGE OF IDEAS
IS TO IDENTIFY,
MANIFEST, AND
SHARE YOUR
CREATIVITY.**

When a product, a person, or an organization radiates creativity, it is very similar. There's no doubt that something special is happening or someone special is present. An emotional reaction takes place that binds the energy of these experiences to your soul and leaves you wanting more, not much different from when you're in love. That's why you sometimes hear people professing strong feelings for their new electronic gizmo, a piece of art, their favorite hotel, an item of clothing, or a great performer. The creative energy that person or product generates makes a tremendous connection with the consumer—so much so that they fall in love with it.

Your creative potential is fully unleashed when you manifest the highest and purest form of your purpose, what you stand for, what you believe in, what you're best at.

Creativity, like love, is entirely emotional, meaning it doesn't have a physical presence. That's what makes it so extraordinary, and yet so difficult for so many to believe in or understand. It makes a lot of very smart people uncomfortable; they have an intense desire for creativity in their lives or businesses, but they can't just purchase it like a material thing or control it like a process in a factory.

To manifest your creativity you must believe deeply in the emotional elements and patiently invest in them. Once you find your creativity, it must be encouraged and enhanced, not controlled. The best of the best—the Apples, Nikes, Michael Jordans, Andy Warhols, Meryl Streeps of the world—have it; they protect it, believe in it, and as long as they stay true to their essence they'll continue to reap the benefits that come with creative thinking and living.

The Value of Creativity

While measuring an individual or organization's creativity is difficult, there's no doubting that the presence of creativity has tremendous value. Consider the following questions:

How much is a two-hundred-dollar Nike sneaker worth if you remove the Swoosh? Twenty dollars? Ten?

What premium would you pay for a pork bun made by David Chang? Sushi made by Nobu? Pasta made by Massimo Bottura?

Why do people pay extra to stay in an Ace Hotel instead of a Holiday Inn? Or fly JetBlue instead of American?

Why does a cotton sweatshirt with a Supreme logo resell on the secondary market for over $500, when they sell at retail for just $125?

Or, at a simpler level, do Windex and Fantastic really clean better than the generic, chainstore versions? Do they clean fifty cents better? A dollar better?

The value of creativity is the difference between the branded price and the commodity price of a product, service, idea, or person.

Branded Price - Commodity Price = Value of Creativity

Let's discuss our Swoosh-less Nike sneaker for a moment. My guess is that if you removed the branding from a pair of Nike Dunk sneakers, they would be worth no more than twenty-five percent of their retail price. That means that at least seventy-five percent of the value of a Nike sneaker is tied up in the emotional elements you can't see or touch, the intangibles. But just because you can't see them or touch them doesn't mean they aren't real.

For a parallel example, let's look at Kanye West's relationship with Adidas. Kanye has little or no athletic prowess—he's a musician, a tastemaker, a hype man. Whatever you may think of Kanye, he gets people talking and has been able to use his brand to create value for his partners. And that's exactly what he did when he designed a line of sneakers for Adidas, the Yeezy Boost.

In February 2015, a limited run of his shoes sold out within ten minutes at a retail price of two hundred dollars. The shoes were then released to a wider audience a month later and once again sold out in record time. This is where things start to get interesting. According to *Complex* magazine, in the following quarter the Yeezy Boost accounted for $2.3 million in sales on eBay, three times the gross sales of its closest competitor, for an average price of $751 per pair. Let's generously assume it cost Adidas fifty dollars per pair to produce and market a pair of Yeezy Boost. If that's the case, Kanye West's creativity is worth $701 per pair, and that doesn't include the halo value to the overall Adidas brand.

That's the value of creativity.

BP - CP = VoC

Branded Price
Minus
Commodity Price
Equals
Value of Creativity

Supreme

The Chanel of downtown streetwear.

—Business of Fashion

When James Jebbia arrived in New York from London in 1983 he had, in his own words, "no training in anything and no loot." He applied for a job at a Soho boutique called Parachute and, lucky for us, he was hired. Jebbia spent five years at the store learning about retail, but like most of us blessed with the entrepreneurial spirit, he eventually started to feel stuck and wanted to work for himself. So he began his own venture, a flea market on Wooster Street, with his then-girlfriend, Maryann.

Around the same time, Jebbia began going back to London regularly. It was on these trips that he was inspired by the "cool and unusual things for young people" at smaller stores like Duffer of St. George and Bond. He recognized that no one was offering that type of thing in New York, so in 1989 he decided to open a shop, Union, featuring English brands that were hard to get in the U.S. He also carried an upstart brand from the West Coast, Stussy, that exploded in popularity and changed everything for Union. When Union got a shipment of Stussy it would sell out instantly, so Union basically transformed into almost a full-on Stussy shop. Through this success, Jebbia befriended the brand's founder, Shawn Stussy, and they decided to open a Stussy-branded store on Prince Street in 1991. The store saw its own share of success, but soon after its opening, Shawn became disillusioned with the direction of his brand, resigned, and decided to sell his shares in the company.

With the future of Stussy unclear, James Jebbia decided to break out on his own once again. He found a vacant storefront with cheap rent on Lafayette Street—then a neglected part of town—and decided to open a store selling what he referred to as "skater stuff." He called the new store Supreme.

Why did he open a skate store? Well, for years he'd been going to fashion industry trade shows like A.S.R. and Magic, and the only thing that excited him there was the skate stuff, which he described as "powerful and raw." He didn't know of any good skate shops left in the city, so he thought that could be a good direction. Jebbia was also personally into the skater graphic decks, tees, and sweats, so he decided to make that the center of his merchandising. What he didn't know at the time was that the stuff he found so personally appealing would become his brand.

While Jebbia may not have written a business plan or had grand aspirations, he did have a very clear vision for what he wanted his store to be: "It needed to be an authentic skate shop that hardcore skaters would appreciate, but just as importantly a shop that people who didn't skate would be intrigued by. And that's pretty much how it went down." Jebbia knew what he didn't know, and in this case he knew he wasn't a skater, so his first and most important hire was Gio Estevez. It was Gio who hired most of the team at Supreme, and he brought in people he knew and trusted: his fellow skaters.

Gio's team legitimized Supreme, and from the first day the store was swarmed by the New York skate community, generating immediate and genuine authenticity. The store's layout helped, with an open central space allowing skaters to enter on their boards. Sales started off slow, with Supreme acting more as a hang-out for skaters than a retail shop. Had Jebbia been shortsighted, he might have killed that vibe, but instead he embraced it because he knew having the skater community would lead to everyone else becoming customers as well. He was humble and smart enough to let his team and core group of skaters take center stage. This fostered the brand's organic growth and enabled him to stay behind the scenes and focus on what he was best at: curating great product (or, as he says, finding "good stuff to sell").

Jebbia's vision and patience paid off. When Supreme started becoming popular, the skaters always came first and everyone else could wait. And since then, that's what everyone else continues to do. Twenty-plus years after their quiet opening, huge lines and crowds are the expectation at Supreme. Moreover, now customers line up and gather not only at the Lafayette Street store but at ten additional Supreme locations, six of them in Japan and the rest in Los Angeles, London, Paris, and Brooklyn. Not only has Supreme collaborated with an eclectic selection of the world's best brands, including Nike, Air Jordan, Comme des Garçons, Vans, Clarks, North

Face, Hanes, Levi's, and White Castle, they have managed to turn skateboards into collectable works of contemporary art.

Supreme has released skateboard decks featuring the work of some of the world's most recognized, relevant artists, including Ryan McGinness, KAWS, Larry Clark, Jeff Koons, Richard Prince, Christopher Wool, Nate Lowman, Damien Hirst, Takashi Murakami, John Baldessari, and Rammellzee. Why would artists whose work sells for millions of dollars make a $150 skateboard design for Supreme? Well, according to Jebbia, "If the project is really good and feels like a good fit, your approach is sincere and you're not trying to screw anyone over, people are quite open to doing things, no matter how large or established they are."

At Supreme they do things their way, with little if any concern for how the rest of the fashion industry operates. Instead of releasing their new collections all at once, Supreme releases a small number of items at a time, usually somewhere between five and fifteen. The "drop," as they call it, occurs online at 11 A.M. local time in America, the UK, and Japan, typically selling out in minutes. While many people believe this strategy is about building hype, the truth is that short runs of product were actually born out of not wanting to saddle their business with excess inventory. The strategy was discovered, not manufactured.

As a result of this strategy, there's now a huge secondary market for Supreme. Do a quick search of Supreme on eBay and you'll understand. The skateboard decks they created with artist Damien Hirst that sold for $150 each in limited quantity are now on sale as a set on eBay for $10,000. And on a recent visit to a consignment sneaker shop in New York, I spied multiple basic-colored jersey sweatshirts with the Supreme logo selling secondhand for five times the retail price less than a month after they were released. There was even a members-only website called Strictly Supreme, where brand zealots traded rumors and merchandise, and invitations to join were almost as hard to get as the clothes themselves. (The site has since shut down and the majority of online reselling has moved to Facebook and Grailed.com.) Once again, this wasn't the result of some contrived marketing strategy; instead, it came out of an obsessive desire to serve the needs of the business and the customer. Says Jebbia: "The most important thing for us is having great products in the store that we hope people will like, that they buy, that sell out, and we keep it moving." Meaning it's far better to make less money but be sold out than to take on excess risk just to increase your short-term profits.

Most businesses have the goal of getting as big as possible. Supreme, on the other hand, strives to remain underground and boutique, growing only when they deem it will enhance the brand. As style writer Glenn O'Brien put it, "Supreme is a company that refuses to sell out." But why? Well, first off, because it wouldn't be authentic to who they are, what they do, and what they're into. For instance, when asked why they wouldn't expand into women's wear, Jebbia simply replied, "It's not what we know." And that's all they've done—manifest an authentic reflection of their core beliefs with unyielding discipline.

Supreme is a reflection of Jebbia's life experiences and passions. It just happened that his passion for "cool and unusual things for young people" was in harmony with the global youth movement that his brand has come to represent. Supreme continues to succeed on a massive scale because they have the discipline to focus their resources on creating great products rather than over-expanding. Or, as Jebbia puts it, "Staying true to what you do best has played a major role in our longevity. I would like people to see that we're a small, independent skate company that has done our own thing, in our own way, over many years, and will hopefully continue to do so."

Art, Commerce, and Authenticity

On the surface, art and commerce aren't clearly connected; if anything, they seem at odds with each other.

Art is the expression of human creativity and imagination, which produces works to be appreciated primarily for their beauty. It's emotional.

Commerce is the activity of buying and selling, particularly on a grand scale. It's black and white: either a purchase is made or it isn't. It's practical.

Prior to the industrial age, commerce was all about fulfilling a need. For example, you need to eat food for sustenance. Therefore, I'll sell you a piece of bread or a glass of beer to satisfy your need. This transaction had no art—one person had the bread or the beer, and the other had the money to pay for the sustenance to survive.

But as time went on, art crept into the equation. There were no longer only one, two, or three entities selling bread or beer, there were dozens, then hundreds, and eventually thousands. And the ones who sold the most made it about more than just fulfilling a practical or commercial need. They took it personally, infusing human creativity and imagination—a/k/a art—into the creation and sharing of their bread or beer.

For example, Wonder wasn't the only industrially produced bread in 1921; it was the only one that was "enriched" with vitamins, pre-sliced, and inspired by the "wonder" of the International Balloon Race at the Indianapolis Speedway. Anheuser-Busch wasn't the first brewery in the United States; it was the first brewery to truly benefit from communicating the advantages of pasteurization, extensive beer bottling, and refrigerated rail cars through advertisements and giveaways such as bottle openers, calendars, and corkscrews. One of these advertisements was a lithograph by St. Louis artist Cassilly Adams. Over a million copies of the print, *Custer's Last Fight*, were distributed, and it's known as "one of the most popular pieces of artwork in American history."

The infusion of art into commerce continues in the modern market. Just think how many artisanal bakers and craft breweries pop up and spread this concept every day. And in our new age, art is more powerful than it has ever been.

Why? Well, as we explained earlier, the ability to reach customers is more cost effective than ever—therefore the intangible and emotional elements have become the key differentiating factor. There are plenty of places to purchase a great spicy tuna roll, but there's only one Masayoshi Takayama. According to his website, "Masayoshi Takayama's appreciation for food started at a young age, growing up working for his family's fish market in a town of Tochigi Prefecture, Japan. From his early years of delivering fresh sashimi to neighbors on his bicycle, to prepping and grilling hundreds of fish courses to cater weddings in high school, his relationship with food has always been a way of life." That's the beginning of a story that makes Takayama's sushi different and special—that makes it art. And that art is what induces people to pay $600 per person in his New York restaurant for a chance to try it.

Despite our efforts to be practical and logical, humans remain emotional beings, and we all crave meaningful emotional interaction with other humans. We don't just want meatballs, we want Grandma's meatballs; we don't just want a smartphone, we want to Think Different; we don't just want to go to any old amusement park, we want to go to the Magic Kingdom; and we don't want water, we want artesian water from Fiji. The story, the experience—that's what is critical to creating, and the emotional connection established through that art is what drives commerce in the contemporary market.

Like Ian Schrager and James Jebbia, creators must deeply believe in what they're manifesting in order for others to believe. Today's term of choice for this conviction is authenticity. Walk into any boardroom nowadays and you'll hear executives asking how they can make their products or services more authentic. The challenge is that there's no way to be authentic without actually doing something that's genuine. You must believe in what you're creating and sharing with the world. Authenticity is exactly that—the point at which you manifest your deep beliefs into something tangible. Therefore, in the modern market there's more value than ever placed on the level of belief that creators have in their creation.

The art world gives us a perfect example of this. When artists start out, no one knows who they are or what they do. Despite this, they start manifesting their vision. A painter begins painting and sharing those paintings with the market. Maybe she sells a couple at a low price, or maybe she can't sell any. So what does she do? Somehow she begins to share the story behind her art. Why does she paint? Where did she come from? What's her inspiration? What's the meaning behind her work? Why does she need—not want, need—to paint? And over time people hear her story: some connect with it and others don't, but the ones who do connect, who see a reflection of themselves in her story, become her tribe. Maybe eventually she gets a gallerist, manager, patron, or publicist, and they share her resonant story with even more people, growing her tribe. Then what happens? Though the paintings are the same, by combining the work with an authentic, resonant story, our painter magically creates value and demand for her art grows.

The value of story—of creator reputation—was vividly demon-strated in a social experiment conducted by the street artist Banksy during a 2013 New York residency. This is an artist whose work has sold for as much as $1.87 million at auction. Banksy erected a street stall on a sidewalk bordering Central Park and had a vendor sell his prints for sixty dollars each. He then posted a video of his experi-ment. Footage from a hidden camera captures some of his most iconic images displayed on a table. Tourists and locals meander by. His first sale doesn't come for hours. A woman buys two small works for her children, negotiating a fifty percent discount. Around four in the afternoon, a woman from New Zealand buys two more. A little over an hour later, a Chicago man who "just needs something for the walls," buys four. With each sale, the vendor gives the buyer a hug or kiss. At 6 p.m., he closes the stall, having made $420. In June 2015, one of these stenciled prints, *Love Is in the Air*—an image of a masked protestor throwing a bouquet of flowers—sold for $249,000. How much of the value of Banksy's art is tied up in his name, his global brand?

Visual art is a compelling illustration of the power of story because art serves no practical purpose. Its value doesn't grow because more people need paintings, like we need shovels after a blizzard—it grows because people connect with the artist through the art. The combination of the work and the story make them feel, and when that happens, people take action to satisfy their emotional need—in this case, desire—by buying and sharing the art. And it's occurred this way since the beginning of time, except now the art—the intangibles—have more power than ever before.

Tracy Chapman

Songwriting is a very mysterious process. It feels like creat-ing something from nothing. It's something I don't feel like I really control.

—Tracy Chapman, songwriter

Tracy Chapman was born in Cleveland, Ohio. Deserted by her father, she and her sister were raised by her mother, Hazel. She was a quiet child and liked to be by herself. It was her mother who recognized her love of music and cultivated it from a young age. At the age of eight the future songwriter became captivated by a country music television show, which led her to ask her mother for a guitar. The instrument harmonized with her soul. Quickly developing her strumming and composition skills, Chapman has been writing her own songs on guitar ever since, expressing herself through lyrics and chords.

She grew up in a rough neighborhood. "At times," Chapman remembers, "it was a terrifying place to be." When she was thirteen, her Ohio school system began integrating black and white students. One day, she was attacked, beaten, and almost killed by a group of white students. As she recalls: "They shouted racial slurs at me. I responded to them and they got really pissed off. They turned around and started beating me up. One guy in particular. It was snowing and he knocked my books to the ground." It would get worse. After her own friends had taken off, terrified, Chapman's main assailant reached into his boot and pulled out a gun. "He told me to run," Chapman recalls, "otherwise he was going to shoot me. I don't know why he didn't." Deeply traumatized by the incident, she would later recount that painful day in her music. The event gave her a determination to escape her surroundings. She pursued a scholarship to a Connecticut boarding school, and secured it. Looking back at this critical juncture early in her journey, Tracy Chapman said the move saved her life.

After relocating east, her love for music continued to grow. Following her graduation from the boarding school, she attended Boston's Tufts University and developed a strong local following for her solo shows. Eventually, fellow Tufts student Brian Koppelman, future screenwriter of films and TV shows such as *Rounders*, *Ocean's Eleven*, and *Billions*, discovered Chapman. It was 1987. The son of a man in the music business, Koppelman was "helping organize a boycott protest against apartheid at school, and someone told me there was this great protest singer I should get to play at the rally." He went to see Chapman perform at a coffeehouse. From that moment on, their lives would never be the same. "Tracy walked onstage, and it was like an epiphany," Koppelman remembers. "Her presence, her voice, her songs, her sincerity—it all came across. It was immediately clear to me that she was among the most gifted people walking the earth."

Koppelman connected with the songwriter after her show and told her, "I have been managing bands since I was thirteen, and producing demos, and working in record companies every summer. And I really have worked to be my own person, but you're so extraordinary. I think my dad can help you, and we should find a way to do something together." Chapman responded by saying she would play the rally but wasn't really interested in anything else. She performed at the protest, and when Koppelman heard her, he realized she was even better than he'd thought the night before. He was intoxicated by the honesty of her songwriting—every time she performed people would leave in tears, moved by the music's beauty and emotion.

Koppelman continued attending Chapman's shows wherever she went, finding himself in coffeehouses, lesbian bars, anywhere and everywhere she performed. Chapman kept talking with him, but declined to cut any demos. So Koppelman hatched a plan; he found out that Chapman had recorded some demos at the university radio station for copyright purposes, so he snuck into the broadcast booth and, while his friend distracted the DJ, grabbed a demo and copied it onto a cassette. It contained only one song—"Talkin' Bout a Revolution." Koppelman sent the tape to his dad, co-owner of a large music publishing company, and the older Koppelman immediately flew up to Boston to see Chapman perform. In short order, he signed her to a contract.

Every record label took a pass on Tracy Chapman except one: Elektra Records. They signed her, but had little expectation that her music and image could make her a commercial success. The signing itself surprised Chapman. "I have to say that I never thought I would get a contract with a major record label," she remarked back in 1988. "I didn't think [record] people would find the kind of music that I did marketable. Especially when I was singing songs like 'Talkin' Bout a Revolution' during the eighties.... I didn't see a place for me there." Most of the industry agreed with her assessment. Even once Chapman was signed, more than a dozen producers declined to work on her album.

Eventually producer David Kershenbaum accepted the project. Chapman's greatest concern was that the integrity of her songs remain intact. "She said right off the bat that she wanted the record to be real simple," says Kershenbaum. "I wanted to make sure that she was in front, vocally and thematically, and that everything was built around her." Every song on the eventual album, with the exception of "Fast Car," was on the original, full-sized demo. Chapman played "Fast Car" during her first meeting with Kershenbaum, and he loved it the minute he heard it, later saying, "It was the most heartfelt song on the album."

The album took eight weeks to record. When they played it for the executives at Elektra, everyone in the room said they loved it. Everyone also thought it wouldn't sell more than 50,000 copies. They couldn't have been more wrong. *Tracy Chapman* was released on April 15, 1988, and went on to sell thirteen million copies. It's ranked No. 10 on *Rolling Stone's* one hundred best albums of the eighties, and that year Chapman won the Grammy for Best New Artist and Best Female Pop Vocal Performance, among countless other accolades.

The beauty, quality, and deeply personal nature of Chapman's music, which had clearly resonated with so many early listeners in Boston, did so in exactly the same way with a large national audience. While she didn't fit into any clear category, the fact that she was different and had manifested a deeply personal message resonated powerfully with the world. Chapman was recently asked what advice she might have given herself when she was starting out, and she responded, "It really is okay to be yourself.... If you are living a life that feels right to you, if you're willing to take creative chances or a creative path that feels like it's mostly in keeping with your sensibilities, you know, aesthetic and artistic, then that's what matters."

Reflect Yourself

Tracy Chapman's music is a reflection of her life experiences, her purpose. Ian Schrager's hotels are a reflection of his life experiences, his purpose. And Supreme's hats and skate decks are a reflection of James Jebbia's dreams and desires. Each of them took their own experiences—the ups, the downs, the good and the bad—and turned them into something sharable, a real-world reflection of themselves. And because it combined their purpose with their singular talent, it flourished.

Jay-Z tells a similar story when describing the journey he took to share his purpose:

My first album [was] called Reasonable Doubt.... It didn't sell massive numbers worldwide. It was still very niche. In my second album [I] tried to make [something that was] bigger and would be more popular, which was a failure. Going for that success really messed up that project and set a bad tone. It was a huge learning lesson for me—that if I was going to be successful I had to be successful at myself.... I had to do what I believed in and what felt real to me and felt true to me. Because the worst thing to be is to be successful as someone else.

Jay-Z went on to say:

I feel sorry for someone who has to walk out the house every day as someone else to make this art and to make something that people connect to. And whatever you have made is not you, you're not happy about it, but it's successful. Just to maintain that level of success has to be very draining and you know a very sad existence because at some point you have to go home. And when you go home all the lights are off and everything is off and you have to look in the mirror and look at yourself and say I like who I am or I am not very happy with who I am. By my third album I had the combination of failing with those pop records and the true and real music I wanted to make. And I blended those two together to make a song called "Hard Knock Life." And that album is when I knew I could do it.

Just like Tracy Chapman, Jay-Z eventually reflected himself in his music. And it worked, both personally and in terms of listener response. As for Chapman's amazing journey, it's worth underscoring again what it illustrates.

Whether it was the kids in Cleveland or record executives in New York, she never allowed them to convince her to be something she wasn't. That fierce commitment to her true self and vision made the music deeply resonate with her audience. She didn't go out and say, *I want to be a star; I want sell a million albums, and make money.* Her aim was to make music that meant something to her, that represented her life experience, and this authentic spirit eventually spoke to millions. In the process, she fulfilled both her internal need to create, and her external need to support her art by selling records.

This core idea of reflecting oneself also applies to the audience. People choose products, services, and, ultimately, brands because they see a reflection of who they are or who they want to be in them. We encountered this with Supreme. Yes, it reflected James Jebbia and the original skaters who worked in his store. But it just so happened there were numerous people with similar values and aspirations who grew up enjoying street style and skate culture. And they chose Supreme because they saw parts of who they were or who they wanted to be in the brand, what it stood for, and how it felt. The more people identify with that energy, the more the energy expands. When a product is a pure reflection of a founder's core values and the customer *feels* that energy, they're attracted to that product.

We're tribal beings. We build our identities through the people and communities we choose to associate with. There's no difference between an ancient tribe tattooing its members with unique symbols and a young person wearing a Supreme T-shirt to associate with the tribes of street style and skate culture. It all comes from the same place, and it's critical that we recognize this behavior so we can apply it to the sharing of our own creations.

Your highest calling is to manifest a reflection of what makes you special.

And then share that reflection, be it a product, a service, a brand, or a work of art, with people who aspire to similar wants, needs, and desires. You reflect yourself in your creations, and they reflect themselves in their consumption and self-expression. The combination leaves both sides fulfilled. In a world where human creativity is the last remaining sustainable, competitive advantage and the principle driver of value creation, your most potent weapon is you. Or, as Oprah explains, "There is no greater gift you can give or receive than to honor your calling. It's why you were born. And how you become most truly alive."

It's Not Business. It's Not Personal.
It's All Emotional.

Your job as a leader is to tap into the power of [a] higher purpose—and you can't do it by retreating to the analytical. If you want to lead, have the courage to do it from the heart.
—Gail McGovern, CEO, American Red Cross

Employees are people. Customers are people. Same for entrepreneurs, business leaders. Conclusion? Companies are created by people and run by people, to service the needs and wants of people. Despite this fairly obvious observation, we tend to manage business and personal matters differently.

For instance, you might have deep empathy for your child or family at home but not have empathy for your employees at work. Or, you know from your personal life that you're at your best when feeling passionate about a project, but you regularly take on business opportunities you or your company aren't passionate about, purely for financial gain.

And individuals often are deeply spiritual or creative in their free time but don't apply those same values or skills in the workplace. It's only rational to think that what brings you success and fulfillment in your personal life will also bring you success and fulfillment at work. Therefore, all the ideals I espouse are applicable to both your business and personal lives, because both are made up of people.

The more I research the emotional elements, the more I realize the divided approach—life on one side, business on the other—is not only ridiculous but harmful to the bottom line. Most individuals run their lives focused solely on meeting their financial needs, and most organizations make decisions based solely on their P&Ls. Traditionally, little or no value is placed on understanding the emotional elements. But in the modern market, it's creativity—a purely emotional element—that has the ability to change the value of a business simply by altering its perception or usage.

But this truth isn't limited to business—the same concept applies to individuals. Once we've met our basic needs—safety, security, sustenance, and shelter—those same emotional elements, not material wealth, determine our level of fulfillment, or, as some may refer to it, our personal success. These parallel truths—that amazing achievement and lasting fulfillment for both individuals and organizations come from understanding and harnessing those emotional elements—are critical to flourishing in our new age, the Age of Ideas.

For example, the creation or ongoing success of a product is entirely dependent on its ability to influence people's actions, primarily by getting them to make a purchase or use a product. Just think of the Internet, which is designed to get you to take a specific action, such as consuming content, making a purchase, or filling out a lead form. Not a single webpage exists without this intention. And the influencing of people's actions is based on impacting them emotionally. We're all emotional beings. To manage, sell to, parent, support, or lead people, we must understand and value the emotional as much as if not more than the practical. Only when you accept and embrace this fact will you be able to fully unlock your potential.

The Myth of Success

A few years ago my therapist asked me, "What do you want out of life?"

I said the first thing that came to my mind: "I want to be successful."

He looked at me, puzzled, and replied, "What do you mean?"

"You know what I mean," I said. "I want to be successful. I want to be wealthy, powerful, and recognized." In other words, I framed a conventional vision of success, the one drummed into us by popular culture and other social dimensions.

My therapist chuckled at my naïveté for a moment and then asked, "Alan, why do you believe that wealth, power, and recognition are the definition of success?" He then went on to explain to me that success is defined as "accomplishing an aim or purpose," but the definition of that aim or purpose is up to the individual.

My mind was officially blown.

AMAZING ACHIEVEMENT AND LASTING FULFILLMENT COMES FROM UNDERSTANDING AND HARNESSING THE EMOTIONAL ELEMENTS.

Up until that day, I had never really thought about why I defined success that way—instead, I'd been obsessed with how I would attain those things. That focus on the how instead of the why had really tripped me up. It had led me to make some very bad decisions and to experience some very unhappy times. When you follow the influence of mainstream culture—television, movies, magazines, and more—to elevate the goals of wealth, power, and recognition above all else, it becomes logical to take selfish or negative actions in order to attain them. After all, that kind of approach—playing the game, playing for keeps, as they say—is put forth as the way to achieve success and happiness. Machiavelli's writings are often referenced to support this point of view—statements like "the ends justify the means"—but it should be noted that Machiavelli died alone and in exile.

It's only when you free yourself from external definitions of success that you're able to comprehend the folly of this type of pursuit. Ask yourself: What's the point of attaining a goal if it isn't going to satisfy your internal needs? All you're going to end up with is some form of a trophy (money, a big house, a nice watch, some press clippings) alongside a big bowl of unhappiness and dissatisfaction. You can only define yourself as a success if the result of your actions is the satisfaction of your internal desires, not that of some superficial, outside force.

It isn't relevant if society deems you a success—it's whether you believe you're achieving success that matters. For some this may mean fame and fortune, but for others it may just mean putting food on the table every night for their family and having a loving relationship with their spouse. The determining factor is how you feel and what you desire on the inside. The first and most powerful step is realizing you have the power to determine what success looks like for you. Only then can you free yourself from the myth and begin the journey of living your truth.

PART TWO: THE CREATOR'S FORMULA

The Theory of Creativity

Everybody has a creative potential and from the moment you can express this creative potential, you can start changing the world.

— Paulo Coelho, author, *The Alchemist*

The greatest challenge individuals and organizations will face when attempting to manifest their creative potential is not a lack of talent or resources—it's a lack of understanding. Even when people believe in the intangibles, they don't understand how they function, or they significantly undervalue them. That puts those who do understand in the precarious position of needing to change people's opinions before getting support—not an easy task. While it is well documented that individuals and organizations that achieve greatness think independently, achieving your goals while fighting constant opposition takes a combination of bravery, confidence, and perseverance that is difficult to develop and exhibit consistently.

It was my own frustration in constantly explaining the value of intangibles that led me to write down these thoughts, intending to increase understanding by creating a coherent explanation of this transformative perspective. The next step in that process is to create a simple framework that can guide individuals and organizations on their journey to unlock their creative potential—what I call the Creator's Formula. It's a set of skills and conditions that must be in place for you to realize this value. The first step is to gain a clear understanding of what each of the elements are and how they work. Then you can begin experimenting with the formula. This will help you build trust in your creative process and eventually harness it for your individual or organizational benefit.

Like most formulas, it requires an investment of time and energy to understand the subject matter behind the formula presented. For example, Einstein's theory of relativity, e=mc2, means nothing without a basic knowledge of physics and mathematics. In our case, the more self-aware you become and the more you practice the art of manifesting—making the intangible tangible—the more effective the formula will become. Think of it as your guide to the process of discovering and sharing the best version of yourself or your organization. A guide that gives you permission to experiment, trust your instincts, and, most importantly, take the right chances that will lead to previously unimaginable results and fulfillment.

The Creator's Formula is made up of four key elements: defined purpose, experienced creativity, flawless execution, and emotional generosity.

We've already seen it at work in the stories of Supreme and Ian Schrager.

Now it's time to explore the formula in detail, illuminating the four key elements, while meeting other creative people whose vivid journeys embody the real-world application of the formula.

THE CREATOR'S FORMULA

Purpose

The why behind everything you do. What drives you, what makes you different, your essence.

Experienced Creativity

The ability to manifest your breed of creativity consistently over a sustained period of time.

Flawless Execution

When a product or service is the ideal manifestation of its purpose.

Emotional Generosity

Understanding the needs of others and being willing to put them ahead of your own selfish desires.

=

Personal Fulfillment & Professional Achievement

Purpose

A master in the art of living draws no sharp distinction between his work and his play; his labor and his leisure; his mind and his body; his education and his recreation. He hardly knows which is which. He simply pursues his vision of excellence through whatever he is doing, and leaves others to determine whether he is working or playing. To himself, he always appears to be doing both.

—Lawrence Pearsall Jacks, philosopher

The secret to a fulfilling life is to discover what excites you, what you love to do, and then spend your days passionately pursuing, sharing, and manifesting that purpose with all your heart. And purpose is exactly that—it's "the reason for which something exists." It's the why behind everything you do. But despite the fundamental importance of purpose, most individuals and organizations are not fully in touch with it, and, worse, have no conscious desire to figure it out.

This is because most organizations are focused on practical elements—what they do ("we sell gym equipment") and how they do it ("through our website and retail stores"). But what really unlocks your creative potential is getting in touch with the purpose behind what you're doing. Author Simon Sinek describes this beautifully in his TED Talk "How Great Leaders Inspire Action," stating that "Instead of asking, 'WHAT should we do to compete?' the questions must be asked, 'WHY did we start doing WHAT we're doing in the first place, and WHAT can we do to bring our cause to life considering all the technologies and market opportunities available today?'"

In today's market, anything that isn't differentiated through creativity or a 10x technology will be immediately commodified by the industrial system. The only way to sustainably incite your audience to take action is to inspire them with meaningful purpose. This makes purpose the holy grail of unlocking your creative potential.

Once you discover your purpose, the goal becomes to live it in all aspects of what you do. This is the integrated life, a life in which there's no difference between work and play; there's only your purpose and what you're doing at that very moment to live that truth, wholly and completely. The closer you get to that point, the closer your entire life comes to being an actualized existence, and the more likely you will enjoy many more of Maslow's peak experiences.

For an example of manifesting through purpose, let's look at the restaurant group Sweetgreen. Founded in Washington, D.C., in 2007 by three college students, Sweetgreen is a fast-casual restaurant chain that describes itself as "a destination for delicious food that's both healthy for you and aligned with your values." The Sweetgreen statement continues, "We source local and organic ingredients from farmers we know and partners we trust, supporting our communities and creating meaningful relationships with those around us. We exist to create experiences where passion and purpose come together."

Notice how the messaging combines what Sweetgreen does practically with what it does emotionally? The last line informs readers that Sweetgreen's goal is to "connect people through experiences that combine passion and purpose." While Sweetgreen specializes in serving healthy salads and grain bowls, there are dozens of salad and health food restaurant groups that do the same. It is Sweetgreen's commitment to their higher purpose that sets them apart.

Through this purpose Sweetgreen has become more than a restaurant—it's become a movement and a community, one that people are so proud to be a part of that they share Sweetgreen content on their social feeds and wear T-shirts emblazoned with the restaurant's logo. The founders remain committed to their differentiating core values, such as "creating solutions where the company wins, the customer wins, and the community wins," and have used those values, rooted in their purpose, to drive the company forward. This led Sweetgreen founders to make choices that weren't always necessarily best on a short-term financial basis but which aided the business and its stakeholders over the long term. For example, when their second store wasn't performing well, the founders purchased a giant speaker, placed it outside facing a park, and threw a block party. They played great music while handing out menus and building individual relationships with community members. This approach, driven by sharing their love of food and music with their community through an experience that combined passion and purpose, eventually led to an annual multiday concert series, the Sweetlife Festival. 2017's festival was attended by 20,000 Sweetgreen devotees and, even better, all the proceeds went to benefit their "Sweetgreen in schools program," which teaches local kids about health, fitness, and sustainability.

The crowds aren't coming to Sweetgreen stores and the festival simply for great salads or cool music acts. They're coming because they buy into what Sweetgreen stands for, and because, on a deeper level, they feel a reflection of themselves in Sweetgreen's purpose—which is itself an honest manifestation of what the people behind the business believe and what they stand for.

Now that you understand what purpose is and why it's important, ask yourself these questions: Who are you? What makes you, you? Why do you do the things you do? What's important to you? What defines you? When you have nothing else going on, what are you thinking about? If money or resources weren't an issue for you, what would you do? What's unique about the way you perceive the world? What did you enjoy doing naturally, before the world began telling you what you should be doing? Who did you need to be to receive the love of your parents? These questions will start you thinking about your purpose, and we'll complete this process of discovery in part three of this book.

Until then, let's explore the next component of our formula: experienced creativity.

Experienced Creativity

Make them laugh, make them cry, make them say 'oh shit.' These are the three things done by creative.

—Harry Bernstein, founder, The 88

Creative agencies are as ubiquitous as coffee shops. Ask any unemployed millennial about their aspirations and don't be surprised if they say they'd like to start a creative agency. In a world where the tools to create and share are available to everyone, the definition of what makes creative work high quality and effective has become unclear. After all, if you have a novice understanding of Photoshop, a Squarespace account, and a few hundred social followers, you can start your very own creative agency right now. While this shift is wonderfully empowering, like all blessings, it's also a curse. Creative work presented without consideration is our kryptonite. It feeds the skepticism and lack of understanding surrounding the value of creative work. Manifesting creativity consistently requires a more refined skill set and approach, one developed over time through practices and systems similar to those of a great athlete, trader, or violinist. I call this brand of creativity experienced, and define it as the ability to manifest consistent, high-quality creative outputs over a long period of time.

As a chief marketing officer, it's my role to source, hire, and manage creative agencies. This gives me a unique perspective on how these entities operate and what differentiates the greats from the not-so-greats, the experienced creative from the amateur free-lancer. The democratization of creative and communication tools has made the ability to define and determine the value of creativity extremely difficult. But the ability to differentiate the good from the bad and find the experienced creativity is a critical element of the Creator's Formula.

Harry Bernstein is an experienced creative. He's been chang-ing the world with his mind quietly and consistently for years. Harry—or Harry Bee, as he's known—is the chief creative officer of Havas New York, an agency that acquired him along with his digital agency, The 88. Harry is deeply intelligent, highly emotional, and overwhelmingly passionate. His speech is quick and choppy, as his mouth struggles to keep up with his mind. His heavy New York accent is a clue to his deep connection with the people and culture of the city. In recent years, all this has blended with marriage and fatherhood to make Harry his best creative self. His years of struggle both personally and professionally have produced a polished gem, a New Age digital philosopher using content, strategy, and creative expression—plus colorful clothing and a substantial beard—to share his beliefs with his myriad followers.

Harry and his team were a major force in the return of Adidas to relevance, launching the incredibly successful NMD line and oversee-ing the marketing for the Adidas Originals brand. He has also applied his talents to Coca-Cola, W Hotels, Belvedere Vodka, Bloomingdale's,

Y-3, the CFDA, Supreme, Pace Gallery, and L'Oréal, among others. But he wasn't always a cultural rainmaker. Harry started out as the child of blue-collar parents in Queens, New York. His father drove a truck for the Department of Sanitation and his mother was a secretary for the Department of Education. Harry got a lucky break his senior year of high school when he got accepted into a program giving him "real-world experience" at an advertising agency. From there, he went to the Fashion Institute of Technology and the School of Visual Arts to continue developing his creative skills.

Prior to starting his own agency, Harry worked for over a decade in the agency world. "I began my career in traditional advertising," he tells me. "In '99, I worked at Ogilvy & Mather, which is a very big ad agency, working on clients like IBM and AMEX. Very blue-chip stuff. Then I quit doing traditional advertising and worked at Berlin Cameron, a small agency, working on things like Boost Mobile. We did a lot of stuff with rappers—Young Jeezy, Fat Joe, Eve. I did Vitamin Water's first TV campaign before they were bought by Coke. My final big client there was Belvedere Vodka, and I did a campaign with Vincent Gallo. After Belvedere, I wanted to try something different. I was actually in Atlanta with Young Jeezy. We were talking about Belvedere, and he was like, 'Harry, my fans don't care about ads. My [followers] look at me in the club. [Me] drinking Belvedere in a club—that's going to do more for you than a TV commercial. They want what I do, not what's in these ads.' I thought, 'Oh, that's interesting.' I had never thought of it that way."

In 2010, Harry decided to launch his own agency, aiming to capitalize on the potential of the digital landscape, specifically combining content and strategy with digital distribution channels to "identify trends in consumer behavior and align brands with them. Building brands within culture, not outside of culture."

If you met Harry in the first half of his life, the success he's now discovered wouldn't have been entirely predictable. He has always been different, testing what worked and what didn't for him. Harry has always stood out by embracing his true self. He's made a conscious choice to be himself above all else, something reflected in how he operated his agency, which featured on-site farmers markets to encourage healthy-eating for employees, and holiday parties with performances by classic rappers like Mase and

Ja Rule. As his mentor Richard Kirshenbaum explained it, "One of the first great lessons I ever learned about being creative is that if you don't embrace who you are and bring your own accent or flavor to your work, you can never truly be creative, authentic, or original." Without a doubt, Harry is an original.

While this may have been one of the first lessons Harry learned, he's learned many others over twenty years as a creative professional. And those lessons, that dynamic process, mark the difference between basic creativity—a talent we all possess—and experienced creativity: the ability to consistently and professionally manifest creative output over a long period of time.

You see, every creative project Harry worked on was a lesson, one that made him more attuned to the subtleties of his process and the needs of his work and clients. He began to intuitively recognize the types of people he wanted on a project, how to deal with people who just didn't get it, and when to open his brain to relaxation so he could welcome new ideas and inspirations. And as he became more attuned to those needs, his brain became better at putting the pieces together and connecting seemingly unrelated elements into new ideas. He also became better at putting together the elements and people who would create the best conditions for unlocking the value of ideas.

Harry shared with me the secret to his creative success, what he feels has helped him evolve into an experienced creative: mindfulness, inspiration, sacrifice, and empathy. These make up the core of his creative practice and have helped him hone his vision and quiet his insecurity. They've enabled Harry to "build a life that creates the opportunity to do great work." As Harry says, "What you put in, you get out," so your inspiration—which he describes as what you consume through your ears, your eyes, your nose, your mind, and your mouth—must be considered, because it's the fuel for whatever it is you intend to put out in the world.

Harry combines this "inspired consumption" with a mindfulness practice that helps him connect more deeply to his inner self. He meditates, which allows him to be "more in the moment and connected," to get more out of his interactions. "Without meditation, I think you are just a robot. You aren't absorbing anything, you're just reacting to messaging being pounded against your eyes,

BUILD A LIFE THAT CREATES THE OPPORTUNITY TO DO GREAT WORK.

ears, nose, mouth and tongue. Focusing on that, and grounding myself—things start to stand out more."

Harry combines these pillars in practice with sacrifice and empathy. Another one of his advertising mentors, Michael Ian Kaye, founder and creative director of Mother New York, taught Harry the value of sacrifice. Kaye used to tell Harry, "Do what you have to do to do what you want to do." Harry explained to me that he feels you must give things up in the short term to get what you want in the long term. There's no gain without sacrifice—you'll never do the work you truly want to do if you don't develop the skill set you need today.

This led Harry to the heart of his philosophy, the notion that "ideas come in the doing: learn it, to know it." Your experiences, in other words, have a significant impact on your ability to create great work, to expand what you're capable of. You don't have to do every job every day, but you must experience something a few times to deeply understand what's going on and how to make it better. For example, you can't communicate effectively with a designer if you can't understand the designer's perspective, and you can't sell sneakers on the streets of New York unless you yourself have spent time buying and selling sneakers on the street. To understand the perspective of another person, you must empathically experience their world; you must connect to their emotions and walk a moment in their kicks.

Like shooting a basketball or playing a guitar, being creative—the miracle of forming something new and valuable through action or thought—must be practiced, no matter what the medium of expression. In studying the formation of exceptional skill, author Malcolm Gladwell was struck by the colossal amount of practice, close study, and emotional dedication that went into developing greatness. He came up with the 10,000-Hour Rule—his estimate for the number of practice hours the masters of a chosen skill, art, or sport put in before they become world-class.

Even child prodigies log countless hours and exhibit extraordinary focus. Michael Jackson didn't just wake up one day and create 13 number-one hits and sell 400 million records. Wolfgang Amadeus Mozart didn't just produce 600 works overnight and suddenly become the most prolific and influential composer of the classical era. They learned and they worked, they failed, and eventually they reached a level of success that has ensured their work would stand the test of time. When I refer to experienced creativity as a critical part of manifesting your ideas, I'm pointing to the need for creativity that has been steadily practiced through years of experimentation; whether or not you're a prodigy, that's what it takes to reach your potential.

Experienced creatives develop the ability to manifest their breed of creativity consistently over a period of time. Simply put, it's the difference between a one-hit wonder and Michael Jackson. A person might get lucky once—come up with a great idea, write a great line, hum an interesting tune—but to manifest your creative potential, you must be able to produce consistent creative results over time. The secret recipe for this phenomenon is to develop your systems and instincts while still being able to see the world with the naïveté and wonder of a child. You must have all the information available but be willing to go against the prevailing wisdom, to be wrong at times, to embrace your fear, or, as my wife says, to "not give a fuck."

Being an independent thinker is the opposite of what we're taught by most organized groups, from preschool classes to our teams at work. We feel comfortable in communities, so we encourage the group dynamic and fitting-in above individuality. But creativity and innovation require that you trust yourself and go against the group—that you think for yourself. Nothing truly innovative, visionary, or creative has ever come out of a group of people sitting in a boardroom giving their opinions on an idea, especially when the market is demanding authenticity. As Harry explains: "Build your own world. I don't care about the numbers game.... Most of the people copy and emulate to get popular. As a young professional creative, don't go for the numbers, create your own point of view."

Trusting yourself enough to go against the grain, to do something that's truly a reflection of your purpose, isn't what we're taught. It only comes when we've gained enough experience to choose our own path, trust our instincts, and create from within. That's what it means to be an experienced creative.

Flawless Execution

There's really no secret about our approach. We keep moving forward—opening up new doors and doing new things—because we're curious. And curiosity keeps leading us down new paths. We're always exploring and experimenting. At WED, we call it Imagineering—the blending of creative imagination with technical know-how.

—Walt Disney

Lillian Disney could sense something big brewing in early 1952. It was one of those times, she would say, when "Walt's imagination was going to take off and go into the wild blue yonder and everything will explode." Walt began liquidating long-held family assets, borrowing against his life insurance policy, selling properties, and even selling the rights to his own name. Walt Disney was planning something new—he was planning to kick down the walls dividing his movies and real life.

When Disney's children were very young, he'd tried to take them to places where their imaginations could run wild. But every carnival or fair seemed to be dirty, poorly run, and filled with vice. Walt wanted to create a place where people could take their family and forget the concerns of the everyday world—a place beautiful, safe, and filled with endless wonder. So at about the same time that he had started selling assets and conserving his capital, he pulled aside one of his art directors and had him begin working on concept sketches for a new kind of amusement park. The sketches started to illustrate the vision he had in his head, a utopian world where guests would enter a fairytale world.

Ever since his early days as a Kansas City artist and animator, Walt had a unique belief in the power of his thoughts. As time went on, he became expert at manifesting his dreams into physical forms, often creating the necessary technology as he went. But nothing prepared him for the challenge of manifesting Disneyland—taking the imaginary world of his movies and making it literally concrete. Disneyland would transport visitors into a captivating three-dimensional story, a sprawling material incarnation of a wonderland that began as a vision, then lived on screens.

Disney knew little about the experiential side of entertainment; his expertise and success was in storytelling through the mediums of animation, film, and television. To make his dream world a reality, Disney chose some of the studio's most talented individuals, took a small building on the Disney lot, and formed a new company, WED Enterprises—an acronym for Walter Elias Disney. This interdisciplinary dream team would be tasked with creating the design, development, and construction of Disneyland—not only doing something that none of them had done before, but that no one had done before. They represented an extraordinary group of storytellers, engineers, animators, contractors, directors, writers, artists, set designers, lighting designers, sound engineers, and many others. WED employees would interpret the Disney stories by building beautiful sets and giving them the interactivity and resilience to wow thousands of guests daily.

The plans for the 160-acre site called for 5,000 cubic yards of concrete and a million square feet of asphalt. The designs included a replica of an 1800s main street, manmade riverbeds for steamboats and jungle cruises, a mile of railroad tracks, and a full-scale Bavarian castle. Walt was at the construction site pushing the WED team every day, giving his attention to every detail, every blade of grass, every leaf on every tree. As former Disney executive vice president and Imagineer Marty Sklar remembers, "The thing we worked so hard to avoid is letting people out of the story with discordant details.... Even the trash cans in the park are for that particular story or theme." The attention to detail and level of execution were extraordinary. "His animations," Sklar recalls, "created a perfect and artificial world, and what he was really doing was making that material in Disneyland. He always thought of Disneyland as a living animation, a living movie, and he thought that people would love to enter a film, not just watch it."

Just like the final cut of a movie before it's released to theaters, Disneyland had to be perfect. The day before the park opened, one crew was trying to dig out a 900-pound mechanical elephant that was sinking, another put lead weights onto a train so it wouldn't tip over when riders came on board, and Walt himself spray-painted backdrops for the 20,000 Leagues Under the Sea exhibit. No detail was too small. The park officially opened on July 17, 1955, with the biggest, most ambitious live-television broadcast ever. The next day, people began lining up to be first through the gates. Disneyland drew a million visitors in its first ten weeks; within two years it was drawing five million visitors annually. In 2017, it drew 18.3 million people.

The WED team—now known as the Imagineers—had combined their moviemaking acumen with hard work and ingenuity to prove firsthand what the watchers of their films had always believed—if you dream something, it can come true. They had transformed an orange grove into the Magic Kingdom by combining Walt's purpose with a wealth of experienced creativity and flawless execution. The Imagineers had made the magic real.

Today, the Imagineers continue to combine their storytelling ability with innovative technology to create magic, holding over one hundred patents in special effects, ride systems, interactive technology, live entertainment, fiber optics, and advanced audio systems. Disney Theme Parks have introduced a multitude of technological landmarks such as Audio-Animatronics and computer-controlled thrill rides. While the Imagineers have an explicit mandate, tremendous resources, and the freedom to combine purpose, creativity, and execution that some creators may never have, it's the simplified principles we learn from their work that matter most. What would happen if you were on a ride at one of the Disney parks and there was a glitch in the system? Or you had a poor food experience at one of the restaurants? Immediately, the glow they worked so hard to create would begin to fade. And that perspective applies to all creative endeavors. If you're an amazing writer but you don't spellcheck or post regularly on your blog, you aren't executing. If you're an amazing chef but you can't scale your cooking to work in a restaurant, catering operation, or some meaningful platform for sharing, you aren't executing. If you're a filmmaker but can't seem to complete a film, then you aren't executing (and, really, you aren't a filmmaker).

The fact is, your creative potential is unrealized without execution. You love Apple products not only because they're beautiful, you love them because they work really well. You love your favorite restaurant not only because the food is great, but because it's consistently great. A product, a brand, and even a person—think of those you know—whenever you have an interaction with one of these entities, they're setting expectations. Whether or not they live up to those expectations determines whether your feelings toward them are good, bad, or indifferent.

Once again, our story comes back to the most simple human interactions. Do you provide more or less value than you promise? Do you live up to your commitments? Do you deliver on your promises? Are you a flawless executor? Or, as Bob Iger, chief executive of Disney said about Walt and his Imagineers, "Walt set a standard early on with the Imagineers. There was a standard that enabled people to come in expecting something and then giving something even beyond that. So they left thinking, How did Disney do that?" Walt Disney always lived up to his word, he always tried to exceed expectations, and he always backed up his dreams with execution. That's why he was able to share so much of his creativity with so much of the world.

Note: Our story about Disney and impeccable execution comes with an asterisk. Your need to flawlessly execute must never come before your desire to create something truly special. More often than not, executors or operators overestimate the importance of mistake-free execution and sacrifice the soul of the idea or the purpose of the organization just to make sure the trains run on time. That's never okay. Think of managing this process as if it's a triangle: on the top of the triangle is Walt, the visionary; the Imagineers, the creatives, are in one of the angles; the Disneyland operations team are in the other. The job of the creator—in this case Walt—is to manage both sides of the triangle in order to ensure that the vision is never compromised. This is done by balancing the decision-making power and enabling an honest and open dialogue that ensures all decisions favor the preeminent manifestation of purpose.

Emotional Generosity

There is a wonderful mythical law of nature that the three things we crave most in life—happiness, freedom, and peace of mind—are always attained by giving them to someone else.

—General Peyton C. March, U.S. Army Chief of Staff

Michael Bonadies is my mentor; sometimes I call him my work father. He's a big man, well past six feet, burly, bearded, energetic. He has three sons, wrote a book on wine, opened a ton of restaurants and hotels (including the legendary Nobu), and has a lovely wife named Anne, who happens to be of Persian descent, like mine. While these aspects describe him, what defines Michael is that he cares. You feel that generosity of spirit when you're part of his world. Through actions, not words, Michael is there for me, and I know I can count on him, in both good times and bad.

I met Michael years ago as an intern for the Myriad Restaurant Group. Myriad, a company Michael founded with Drew Nieporent, was the forerunner to many modern restaurant groups throughout the world today. From one restaurant, Montrachet, sprang dozens, most of them star-studded, with partners like Robert De Niro and investors like Bill Murray and Sean Penn. As a student at Cornell, I'd read about Michael's restaurants, heard his partner speak, and wanted in on the action. I landed a spot in their coveted management training program and got some brief exposure to Michael's world. Fast forward a decade, when our paths crossed again: this time I was the one running the company and Michael was the consultant.

Knowing I had come through Myriad, Michael relished seeing my success and began coaching me through every step of my growth. He helped me with lessons from his journey and gifted me with the confidence to trust my instincts and follow my dreams. Michael made himself available for countless breakfasts, lunches, late-night phone calls, and text messages, and also was in the front row at my son's bris, provided me pointers on creating a healthy marriage, and took my wife and me to dinner. I can say without a doubt that I wouldn't have been as successful in my career or my life had it not been for Michael's love and support.

It's interesting to note that Michael doesn't only mentor me; he's a mentor to dozens of the biggest names in the hospitality business, not to mention to his own children. And while sometimes he's paid for his services, more often he isn't. Either way, he always makes the people he cares about feel important. He takes the time to know them and makes sure they know he cares. That unique ability—to wrap his heart around you and make you feel that what you're dealing with is the most important thing in his world—is something only someone with emotional generosity can do, and Michael embodies that magical power.

Emotional generosity is when an individual or organization combines empathy—the willingness to feel, understand, and share another person's experiences and emotions—and sacrifice, surrendering something you need or desire so that someone else can have it. The result of combining these two attributes is trust: the belief that someone or something is good, honest, and reliable. And when someone trusts you, they're willing to emotionally connect with you. That connection, that bond, is invaluable, both in personal relationships and organizational loyalty and growth. When people feel trust and connection, they allow themselves to be taken on a journey, and that's what makes it possible to create something truly special.

Let's dive a little deeper. Take a moment and think of your most selfish acquaintances. Do you trust them? Absolutely not. No one wants to be friends with someone who's selfish, self-involved, or manipulative. On the other hand, we all want to be friends with someone who's emotionally generous—someone supportive, loving, caring, and connected. As mentioned earlier, organizations are no different, because they're made up of and sell to—you guessed it—people. Therefore, in order to manifest the wonderful in your life and business, emotional generosity must be a key part of how you operate, communicate, and think. That explains why actions such as email spamming, chronic discounting, and disconnected customer service aren't effective in the long term. These actions are lazy and show a lack of authentic care and meaningful connection. If you take the time to make a personal call to a client, create content that is deeply creative, or fix something because it's the right thing to do for the customer despite your bottom line, you're being emotionally generous. Shortcuts don't work because by nature they show you don't really care about the customer's needs more than your own. Manipulating a customer into action is no different from manipulating a friend to get your way. True emotional generosity combines action and intention to create lasting connection.

Let's go back to Michael for a moment. While he was there during the good times, it was his presence during tougher times that solidified my trust, loyalty, and respect for him. You see, the first time I was promoted to chief marketing officer, I never received more gifts and cards during a holiday season, ever. I was sent more champagne than I could possibly drink. But a couple of years later, things weren't so rosy, and it was around the holidays that I was going through some real struggles. The gifts that year were far fewer, and Michael was no longer on the receiving end of business from me or my company. But guess what? Michael was more present in my life than ever. He invited me to a holiday lunch with him and his son, he actively coached me on my writing, and he met with me more than he ever did when I was his client. Michael became one of my closest friends.

It was at that point I fully appreciated Michael's generous spirit, his lack of selfish motives. By giving himself to people like me, he gives himself the greatest gift imaginable: Michael fills his world with an energy and fulfillment that will sustain him well beyond his ability to contribute.

And that's the biggest lesson we can learn from Michael, a principle that applies to all individuals and organizations: by generously manifesting your purpose and sharing it without selfish motives, you create things that sustain well beyond your ability to personally contribute.

If that sounds a bit mystical, that's because it is. But let me frame it more practically.

In our new paradigm, your business must make people feel. The people who need to feel good about your brand are your customers, and your job is to make them happy. Customers are happy when they feel you understand their needs and are willing to sacrifice to make sure they're met. This sacrifice can manifest itself in many forms—from working extra-hard to provide the goods or services you promised, or going above and beyond to fix something that went wrong. Whatever you do, when you meet the needs of your customers consistently and exceed their expectations with more care for their happiness than your bottom line, you become worthy of loyalty and trust. That loyalty and trust strengthens the connection that's the bedrock of a great brand and a key component of unlocking your creative potential. That's what it means for an organization to be emotionally generous.

Note: There is such a thing as being too emotionally generous, which can negatively impact the core health of the individual or the organization. For example, if a customer has a negative experience, you may be able to show your care by speaking to them directly or even refunding their check. But if you're consistently refunding checks over a sustained period of time, you either need to fix the service or, if it's just a few consistently problematic people, lose the customer. The same applies to individuals: there are extreme situations in which people give to others without taking care of themselves, and ultimately that is unsustainable. You must always protect the core health of the individual or organization prior to servicing the needs of third parties.

PART THREE: STARTING YOUR JOURNEY

The hardest thing that there is, is to get up in the morning, look in the mirror, and be happy. Everybody wants this, of course, everybody looks for this. I have achieved this. It has been thirty years that I get up in the morning very early. I work sixteen hours doing what I love and I sleep and I am happy. Why? Because I have passion for what I am doing and I have challenges that I always believe I am not going to reach and I fight to achieve them. That is what life is, a struggle to reach a challenge.

—Chef Ferran Adrià

Discovered, Not Manufactured

People are so different. It's almost like you need to go through the process, discover and unlock what it is that makes that band that band. And a lot of times they don't know it.

—Rick Rubin, music producer

In early 2013, Kanye West asked legendary producer and Def Jam Recordings cofounder Rick Rubin to help complete his new album, *Yeezus*. With only days to meet West's deadline and a rough cut of sixteen unfocused and unfinished tracks, the task appeared nearly impossible. West couldn't seem to create the sound he'd imagined, and his process bordered on perfectionism. Though he was certain it would come to him, he had no idea how or when. He needed something, or in this case someone, who could reveal his vision.

When Rick Rubin showed up, the album's rough cut ran nearly three and a half hours. In the studio, the two began deconstructing the tracks, unveiling the "edgy and minimal and hard" sound West had been searching for. The duo worked for sixteen days, fifteen hours a day, with no time off. With just two days left, five songs still needed vocals, and two or three of them still needed lyrics. In a final flurry of remarkable creative collaboration, West and Rubin finished those songs and the album in one two-hour session. The final cut of the album featured ten songs for a total length of forty minutes— less than 20 percent of the original three and a half hours of music. Rubin had broken down West's compositions to their simplest form, leaving only the essence of his ideas, and the results were epic.

When *Yeezus* was released, it debuted at #1 on the Billboard

200 and eventually went platinum. *Yeezus* was the most critically acclaimed album of 2013, appearing on sixty-one Metacritic top-ten lists and named #1 on eighteen of them. Critics commended its brash direction. When asked about their collaboration, Kanye said, "Well, I didn't reduce it. Rick Rubin reduced it. He's a reducer, not a producer."

Rick Rubin

Rick Rubin grew up in Lido Beach, New York, not far from JFK Airport. His father, Michael, was a shoe wholesaler, and his mother, Linda, a housewife. In 1982, during his senior year of high school, he founded Def Jam Recordings and formed a punk-rock band called Hose. Using his high school's equipment, he recorded a Hose track that would eventually become Def Jam's first release. Hose played punk clubs in New York City, the Midwest, and California, but broke up as Rubin's interests shifted more toward hip-hop. In 1994, Rubin and DJ Jazzy Jay of Universal Zulu Nation coproduced Rubin's first hip-hop single, "It's Yours," for the rapper T La Rock. As the song started getting played in clubs and on the radio, Rubin's music found a fan in Russell Simmons, who was making a name for himself as an artist manager and concert promoter. Rubin convinced Simmons to join him at Def Jam, and the pair was soon holed up in Rubin's New York University dorm room, sifting through demos of aspiring rappers in between Rubin's classes on philosophy and film.

In late 1984, Def Jam scored its first hit with LL Cool J's song "I Need a Beat," selling over 100,000 copies. The rapper's first album, *Radio*, would be the first Rubin "reduced," and it would go platinum. Next would be the Beastie Boys' *Licensed to Ill*. It would go ten times platinum, selling over ten million copies, cementing Def Jam's reputation.

Rubin literally didn't miss a beat from there. Def Jam was at the forefront of introducing hip-hop music into popular culture, with the discovery of Run-DMC and Public Enemy. At the same time, Rubin began exploring his own eclectic tastes. He produced an album by heavy-metal band Slayer and followed that by pairing Run-DMC with Aerosmith on the trailblazing track "Walk This Way."

In the late eighties, Rubin decided to head to Southern California. While it was the end of his involvement with Def Jam, it only led to an even bigger impact on the world of music and culture. After his relocation, Rubin produced the Red Hot Chili Peppers, Johnny Cash, the Black Crowes, Jay-Z, Danzig, the Dixie Chicks, Tom Petty and the Heartbreakers, Metallica, AC/DC, Aerosmith, Weezer, Linkin Park, the Cult, Neil Diamond, Adele, System of a Down, Rage Against the Machine, Lana Del Rey, Lady Gaga, Shakira, Ed Sheeran, and Eminem. Producer Dr. Dre described Rubin as "hands down, the dopest producer ever that anyone would ever want to be, ever."

Ironically, if you ask Rick Rubin what a music producer does, he will tell you, "I don't know what music producers do. I can tell you what I do."

So, what is it that Rubin does? How has he helped artists make their best music for nearly forty years across such disparate genres and styles? The secret seems to be rooted in self-discovery. As Natalie Maines of the Dixie Chicks put it, the legendary producer "has the ability and the patience to let music be discovered, not manufactured." In other words, to use our terminology, Rubin understands that magic needs to come from within.

Rubin describes the process similarly: "We try to go on a journey and let the artist discover who they are, and in the process the best art comes from them. It's like getting to be their true selves and trying to take away all of the things [that get in the way]."

This discovery process involves less doing and more listening, which Rubin says is vital to the process. As he explains it, "I'll spend time with an artist and listen very carefully to what they tell me and get them to talk about their true goals, their highest, highest goals. We go back to the heart of why they started doing what they are doing in the first place."

This combination of the internal, intangible emotional journey and the practical skill of making music—the "heartwork and headwork," as Rubin calls it—is how he's sustained his craft across genres for so many decades. He taps into something far beyond the type of music or production style, and instead connects to the artist through a first-principle truth: that their greatest work can only come from manifesting and sharing a reflection of their true purpose. Identifying one's true purpose, and using that knowledge to guide decision-making in life and work, is in fact the first step in the Creator's Formula.

Implementing The Creator's Formula

As Rick Rubin's example illustrates, great work must be "discovered not manufactured." And this process of discovery is to a great extent a searching out of the artist's truest purpose. Likewise, individuals and organizations determined to start manifesting truly impactful work must discover their purpose. In the Age of Ideas, this discovery process is more critical than ever. Consider, for example, the way consumer taste has changed, against the bigger backdrop of the market's evolution beyond the industrial-age model. Today, customers are looking for products and services featuring what the Japanese call "wabi sabi"—things and experiences that have been touched by humanity, that are imperfect and carry a deeper level of meaning in their making. It's the difference between Heinz Ketchup and the craft brand Sir Kensington's Ketchup. Tastes have shifted to the latter—products that are personal, that have a story, that are crafted rather than endlessly, slickly reproduced. That are connected to purpose, not just profit.

Discovery occurs when the creator(s) looks within, and creative outputs improve as self-awareness increases. The more you understand about yourself and what is important to you, the more meaningfully you can share that with the world.

But self-discovery must be combined with the other elements of the Creator's Formula—experienced creativity, emotional generosity, and flawless execution—in order to turn those ideas into personal fulfillment and professional achievement. Who we are to the outside world and whether we are able to manifest our purpose is the result of work done when no one is looking. Every decision we make has positive and negative implications for our future and therefore must involve a strong framework, one that guides our choices and focuses our energy. Enhancing self-understanding and transforming that awareness into fruitful decisions and actions is what part three of this book is all about.

Let's get started implementing the Creator's Formula by doing the "heartwork and headwork" necessary to understand yourself more deeply. Do this, and you're on your way to enabling your best work, output that is purpose-driven, creative, and fulfilling.

IMPLEMENTING THE CREATOR'S FORMULA

"Heartwork & Headwork"

Discovering Your Purpose

Connecting to Your Inner Desires & Setting Your North Star

Integrating Your Life

Achieving harmony between your emotional needs and your everyday existence.

Choosing Your Challenge

Your best choice or best course of action based on your priorities.

Understanding Your Biases

Diminishing negative inclinations or prejudices for or against people and things.

Building Your Wave

The compounding effect of combining good decisions with great execution.

Cultivating Appreciation

Balancing our desire for more with the appreciation of what we have.

Discovering Your Purpose
Creator's Formula: Define Your Purpose

At the center of your being you have the answer; you know who you are and you know what you want.

—Lao Tzu

As Rick Rubin demonstrates and the Creator's Formula explains, to discover your purpose and unlock your creative potential, you must connect to your inner self. But Western culture prefers the world you can see and touch: to "be somebody," you have to look good and have a lot of money. This is an unhelpful message, because your purpose—the factor that has the most impact on your fulfillment—is completely internal. Generally, when someone is unhappy or lacking meaningful sustenance in their life or business, it's because their internal self isn't in harmony with their external self. For example, they love to paint or work with their hands, but spend all day working in an office on finance. While this may be an oversimplification, it's precisely this type of dissonance that causes energy blocks that manifest in people as depression, anxiety, and frustration, and in organizations as poor performance, low engagement, and weak sales. Bottom line, and to quote our friend Mr. West, we "worry 'bout the wrong things, the wrong things."

In simplest terms, you won't be able to unlock your creative potential, achieve sustainable success, or even be fundamentally happy unless you align your internal and external worlds—unless you're true to yourself. Therefore, to begin the journey of discovering your purpose, you must focus on what matters to you internally, not externally. And the first step in this process is to eliminate obstacles that prevent you from hearing the signal above the noise. These obstacles include things such as commercial concerns, financial motivations, comparing yourself to someone else, and other manifestations of ego. Think of the little devils sitting on characters' shoulders in cartoons—that is the exact function of these obstacles, confusing you by telling you the superficial or selfish thing to do. Your goal is to eliminate those voices and learn to concentrate instead on that small voice in the back of your head expressing your true desires and work to slowly build up its presence in your inner narrative. You must encourage your soul-level wants and needs to bubble up to the surface and take center stage.

Let's return for a moment to Rick Rubin and his process with artists.

According to Rubin, "One of the main things I always try to do is to create an environment where the artist feels pretty comfortable being naked—that kind of a safety zone where their guard is completely let down and they can truly be themselves and feel open to exposing themselves. It's very powerful when people do that, when people really open up." And that's exactly what you must do to discover your purpose. Create a safety zone for yourself where you can shut off the world for a moment and ask yourself the important questions, exploring what really matters, without any concern for the implications of those thoughts or decisions. Because if you don't access what exists deep inside you, as Lao Tzu says, you may end up where you are heading without knowing if it's really where you want to go.

Purpose Exercise #1: The Ultimate Question

Now, let's do a quick exercise to begin the journey of discovering your purpose.

Close your eyes and take a couple of deep breaths; try for ten, five will suffice.

Now imagine your time on this earth is coming to an end. A doctor is sitting in front of you telling you it's all over in two weeks, and there's nothing she can do.

Sit with this realization for a moment.

What would matter to you?

What would you want people to know about you?

Take a few minutes to reflect on this question.

Then take five more deep breaths and open your eyes.

Now write down the five things that matter to you most.

Let me start by apologizing if I startled you, but death has a powerful way of cutting to the core of things. I'm pretty sure that most of you didn't think of your car, your clothes, your hair, your bank account, or that you were right in a lot of arguments (unless maybe you're a lawyer). There's no right or wrong when you're dead, and you can't drive around in your Porsche after you're gone. For most people, your thoughts settle on the people you love and the things you've done or do that you're really proud of. Those five things are the first clue in the mystery of discovering your purpose.

Now, let's revisit our definition of purpose: the reason for which something exists. It's the *why* behind everything you do, what drives you, what makes you different. It's your essence, and figuring that out isn't as easy as performing one quick exercise. Listen to Nick Craig and Scott A. Snook, who wrote "From Purpose to Impact" for the *Harvard Business Review*:

"We are constantly bombarded by powerful messages (from parents, bosses, management gurus, advertisers, celebrities) about what we should be (smarter, stronger, richer) and about how to lead (empower others, lead from behind, be authentic, distribute power). To figure out who you are in such a world, let alone 'be nobody but yourself,' is indeed hard work. However, our experience shows that when you have a clear sense of who you are, everything else follows naturally."

Purpose Exercise #2: Self-Discovery Q&A

When we introduced purpose in Part Two, I mentioned some questions—it's finally time to get back to them. These questions are the next step in the process of discovering your purpose and, eventually, refining it into a simple statement.

> *How would you describe yourself? How would your closest friends and/or family describe you?*
>
> *How are you different from your peers? What are your defining characteristics?*
>
> *What motivates you to get out of bed every morning? What do you think about before you go to sleep at night?*
>
> *When you have nothing else going on, what do you think about?*

What would you do if money or resources weren't an issue?

What's unique about the way you perceive the world?

What did you naturally enjoy doing when you were very young, before the world began telling you what you should be doing?

What have been your most challenging life experiences? What did you learn from those experiences? List at least three.

In your life right now, when do you feel most naturally fulfilled? When do you feel the most harmony with the surrounding world?

What do you find easy that many of your friends or colleagues find hard?

Similarly, here's a list of questions for organizations:

What does your company do? How would you describe your company? How would your most senior employees and/or your competitors describe you?

What makes your company unique? How are you different from your competitors? What's your defining competitive advantage?

What do you think motivates your employees to get out of bed every morning?

What's important to your team? List the five most important things to you in priority order.

Why was your company started? What worries you most about the company?

What would you do if resources weren't an issue?

What's unique about the way your company sees the world? Speaks to the world?

What have been your most challenging times as an organization? What did you learn from those experiences? List at least three.

*In what area of the business do things just work; flow nat-
urally? When do you feel the most harmony between the
company and the consumer?*

After you've written down your answers to these questions, ask at
least two people you trust and respect to answer them for you as
well. It is difficult to see who you are fully and completely, so insight
from others you trust will help you fill out a more complete picture
of yourself.

Principles Of Purpose

While your purpose is yours and yours alone, there are a few simple,
universal principles you need to follow in the discovery and formu-
lation of your purpose.

1. The first principle is that your purpose can't be selfish.
   We've touched on this a couple of times already, and it will
   continue to be a recurring theme. One of the key elements
   of the Creator's Formula is emotional generosity, and
   when you are chiefly concerned with your own profit or
   pleasure, you aren't being generous. Putting the needs of
   others ahead of your own desires is a first-principle truth.

For an example, let's look at Ikea's vision statement and extract the
purpose:

*"At IKEA our vision is to create a better everyday life for
many. Our business idea supports this vision by offering a
wide range of well-designed, functional home-furnishing
products at prices so low that as many people as possible
will be able to afford them."*

While making inexpensive furniture may be what IKEA does practically, the vision of "creating a better everyday life" for people has
emotional resonance we can rally behind. These are the words of
a movement, and I would argue that without them, Ikea would be
much less successful. Combine commitment to a meaningful purpose with flawless execution and it makes the difference between
the world's largest furniture retailer and a local purveyor of cheap
junk. That's the power of tapping into your creative potential.

2. The second guideline is that your purpose shouldn't include anything about results. Your purpose is the emotional and spiritual energy that surrounds the commercial aspects of what you do; it can't be to make a lot of money or sell a lot of widgets. While generating a significant financial return may be a result of pursuing your purpose, it can't be why you do what you do. Money isn't what the journey's about. We aren't here to survive; we're here to self-actualize and thrive. Individuals and organizations that unlock their potential are never motivated primarily by financial gain. With that said, manifesting your purpose often results in more wealth than you could ever have imagined—and that's great, because material wealth allows you to continue pursuing your purpose.

3. The final guideline is that your purpose must be authentic and honest. While this should be assumed, it's sometimes difficult to form a consensus purpose, especially in large organizations. Quite often, the discussion of purpose in an organizational setting is diluted by groupthink, as most people don't feel comfortable giving their honest opinion, especially when doing so could impact their employment or financial status. Therefore, organizations must work to find ways to create safe environments for honest sharing and empower key stakeholders to make decisions that aren't always popular—because to do something truly special, you must be as honest, defined, and differentiated as possible. As Shane Smith, founder of Vice Media, said, "If something is created in a boardroom, if something is created by consensus, if something is created by a bunch of baby-boomers who say it will be cool, 'We are going to do skateboarding' or something, it will not work."

The Result: Your Defined Purpose Statement

Once you've compiled your feedback, you can begin to construct a brief but meaningful statement of purpose. A simple sentence—two sentences max—that distills what makes you different and what's important to you. This declaration should begin with "My purpose is _____" and should be written in your own words, encapsulating your essence and summoning action. Let's use mine as an example:

"My purpose is to guide and inspire individuals and organizations in manifesting and sharing their creative potential."

Hence the reason I've written this book!

This statement is extremely important, as it will be your north star. Every decision you make will be primarily measured by whether it is bringing you closer to living the purest manifestation of your purpose, which is captured in this statement. As a business you can look to your purpose statement to analyze strategic plans to see if you are remaining focused on your unifying thread, or that which you can be the best in your world at. Even better, it should be a rallying cry for your people, an idea to inspire them and help them make the best decisions when you are not around.

Mentee Zero: Chad Campbell

To illustrate the purpose-discovery process, let's consider the example of Chad Campbell, one of the first people I mentored. Chad has a huge heart, tons of passion, and, luckily for him, he looks like a combination of Justin Bieber, Brad Pitt, and Grizzly Adams. Born in Kansas City, Chad was rebellious when young, always finding new and different ways to get into trouble and push against authority. Trying to keep him busy, his parents put him to work doing everything from mowing lawns in trailer-parks to fixing cars and laying bricks. They made sure Chad worked hard.

While his upbringing laid the foundation for his humble nature and strong work ethic, it didn't instantly make him a fan of working. When he graduated college, Chad "felt something was missing." He wasn't excited by traditional career paths and started searching the Internet to find something that spoke to him. After googling "the last great adventure," Chad came across a site detailing the Pan-American Highway, a 19,000-mile road connecting Prudhoe Bay, Alaska, with Ushuaia, Argentina.

It's the longest motorable road in the world, according to the people at Guinness World Records, and it piqued Chad's interest.

He set off on a journey to explore the road, to "go where no one he knew had gone before" and to "speak to people no one was speaking to or giving a voice to." With minimal funds and maximum heart, he embarked on an adventure that would last many months, with experiences far too numerous to recount here. After a couple of years on the road, Chad got a call from a friend asking if he wanted to help open a hotel. That's how he ended up in the hospitality business, returning to what Americans call "the real world." His chance opportunity eventually led him to New York City, and into my purview.

When we sat down to explore Chad's purpose, it was in a group setting in my office. He was chafing at the rules the company was trying to impose upon him. By this time, he'd begun to achieve a level of financial success, but he was feeling less and less connected to his daily life. As we explored his purpose, Chad spoke passionately about his trip. He expressed that he'd felt most in his element when he was on "a journey of discovery." He wanted to gain knowledge he felt he couldn't get from teachers, books, or traditional experiences. And he deeply wanted to share these experiences with others, giving voice to overlooked people and places. He wanted to share the beauty he saw, and in the process, transform the thoughts and feelings of people back home, whether that be in New York or Missouri.

All these feelings became the basis for Chad's purpose statement—"to shed light on the unseen parts of the world." These few words connected all the things that drove him internally. They combined his deep desire for discovery, knowledge, and anti-establishment thinking with advocating for those without a voice. He now had a unifying thread, a binding narrative that tied all his life experiences together, and that statement became a beacon in Chad's decision-making processes, providing him with a light to illuminate the many paths and decisions life put in front of him.

Like Chad, we all have primary motivations that exist beneath the superficial elements of life, making us who we are. The key now will be to manifest your purpose in pursuits that are a reflection of that purpose. Whether in your personal life, through who you pick as your spouse or where you vacation, or through the creation of your own business or a job you take, the closer you come to living

WE ALL HAVE PRIMARY
MOTIVATIONS THAT
EXIST BENEATH
THE SUPERFICIAL
ELEMENTS OF LIFE,
MAKING US WHO WE
ARE. THE KEY NOW
WILL BE TO MANIFEST
YOUR PURPOSE IN
PURSUITS THAT ARE
A REFLECTION OF
THAT PURPOSE.

your purpose every day, the more fulfilled and successful you'll be. Your purpose statement is your compass. It's what will guide you home, except this home isn't a place but rather a state of being where you feel most in tune with yourself and the universe.

Integrating Your Life
Creator's Formula: Experienced Creativity

Take it that you have died today, and your life's story is ended; and henceforward regard what future time may be given you as uncovenanted surplus, and live it out in harmony with nature.

—Marcus Aurelius

Velcro was invented in 1948 by Swiss engineer George de Mestral. The miracle material that makes it possible for children to close their sneakers without shoelaces was conceived when he went for a walk in the woods and wondered what he could learn from burrs. Nature made these seed cases prickly for protection and sticky to spread seeds, a combination that made them very difficult to clean off his trousers (and dogs). De Mestral realized he could apply the same design to a synthetic version for industrial use. After years of researching nature's brilliance, he successfully reproduced this natural function by utilizing two strips of fabric—one side with thousands of minuscule hooks and the other with thousands of minuscule loops. The name Velcro came from a combination of two French words, velours and crochets ("velvet" and "hooks"), and it was formally patented in 1955.

Velcro is quite possibly the most famous example of biomimicry. This field of research and innovation is defined as "the design and production of materials, structures, and systems that are modeled on biological entities and processes." Or, simply put, copying nature's brilliance to find solutions to our problems.

When you understand biomimicry, it's very much a why-didn't-I-think-of-that? moment. It's just so obvious. What hubris do we have, thinking our solutions will be more effective than those already in place in the natural world? Why should we know how to capture the sun's energy better than a leaf? Or fly more efficiently than a bird? According to Janine Benyus of the Biomimicry Guild, "We are part of a brilliant planet...surrounded by genius. [Organisms] are doing things very similar to what we need to do. But they in fact are doing them in a way that have allowed them to live gracefully on this planet for [a very long time]."

Before humans started messing around with the system, nature existed in harmony for millions of years—a beautiful symphony of seasonal change, birth and death, creation and destruction. This same harmony that drives the natural world applies to the intangible, emotional world of humans. We, too, must achieve harmony between all the elements of our lives, between the internal self and the external world.

A harmonious state of being is defined as a state in which your internal needs are aligned with the actions you take and the surrounding energy of the world. The only way to create this harmony is by aligning your priorities with what you do every day. This harmony is vital to the manifestation of experienced creativity and flawless execution. To manifest your best work you must create an environment that nurtures and facilitates the focus of your time and energy. While "harmony" may sound very zen, you need to take an active role in manifesting this state of being: you must be intently aware of your own internal state and work tirelessly to remain in sync with your priorities and the world surrounding you.

Core aspects of your life or business that affect harmony are:

For individuals

- Work/School: Where you learn or create

- Home/Family: Who you live with and are related to

- Community/Friends: Who you choose to interact with regularly

- Body/Mind/Spirit: The self

For organizations

- Finances: Revenues/Profits

- Employees/Partners: Key internal stakeholders

- Customers: Those you serve

- Global/Local Community: Surrounding entities you impact

When these key aspects of your existence are in harmony, you'll create sustainable and fulfilling outputs that reflect your individual or organizational purpose, eventually unlocking your creative potential. To do this, to manifest your brand of experienced creativity, you must make decisions that benefit all or most of the areas of your life rather than just one or two.

Let's review a simple example. You get an amazing job offer, but if you take it, you'll have to work so much you'll never see your family. This satisfies the work aspect of your life but puts it in direct opposition to your family. This lack of harmony eventually will manifest itself in a problem or blockage that prevents you from being able to create sustainably. For an organizational example, think of a company that's generating record-setting profits or growth by espousing philanthropic beliefs—promising "one pair of shoes goes to charity for every one sold"—but isn't actually following through with their charitable mission. Eventually, the truth will come out and the profits will slow down or stop altogether.

Sometimes, when we least expect it, energy moves like a tornado, in directions we don't expect and that can feel negative. Our plan and harmony are disrupted, and then the question becomes, what do we do?

The natural reaction when something happens that's unplanned is to panic or "fight the energy." But that's exactly the type of action you don't want to take, because it's in exact opposition to the harmony we're aiming to achieve. So what can we do instead? There's only one answer: accept it. Pause, take a deep breath, and trust that everything that happens is in your best interests.

This is really important. The key to achieving harmony and to manifesting your creative potential is to allow the surrounding energy to take you to where you need to be at that moment in time. You must trust the energy. Instead of fighting where the world is taking you, make an effort to understand why; look inside yourself to see the bigger picture. Maybe you lost a job because you're supposed to move on from it. Or maybe a line of business is failing because you are supposed to shut it down. Maybe you didn't get a house you put a bid on because you are not supposed to buy that house. We're part of an energy system that's much larger than ourselves, and sometimes we can't understand the potential positive outcomes of things we perceive to be negative. We can't understand how this situation is bringing us closer to our ideal reality. In those cases, it's critical to accept that we aren't always in control.

I know, I know; accepting a lack of control is counterintuitive and difficult—but when you realize that fighting the energy only creates chaos both personally and professionally, you'll accept that existing in harmony with nature is the only solution. Or, as the great Roman emperor Marcus Aurelius said, "When force of circumstance upsets your equanimity, lose no time in recovering your self-control, and do not remain out of tune longer than you can help. Habitual recurrence to the harmony will increase your mastery of it." Marcus Aurelius was, in his time, the most powerful man in the world; I promise you, his problems were greater than yours. If he can do it, so can you.

Achieving Integration

Happiness is when what you think, what you say, and what you do are in harmony.

—Mahatma Gandhi

The physical manifestation of harmony is integration. During the time of the industrial system, there was a clear separation for most people between what they did for a living and what they did in their free time. It was universally accepted that work was filled with struggle and sacrifice. The payoff was financial gain and, if you were lucky, a hint of passion on the weekends and leisure during your annual vacation.

The experienced creative, whether playing the role of employee or entrepreneur, must integrate their emotional needs with their everyday existence. And organizations must integrate the emotional needs of all stakeholders, employees, customers, and the surrounding community, into their business model. Dean Kamen, the famed inventor and scientist, tells a beautiful story about his father Jack that perfectly captures the idea of an experienced creative achieving integration:

THE EXPERIENCED
CREATIVE MUST
INTEGRATE THEIR
EMOTIONAL NEEDS
WITH THEIR EVERYDAY
EXISTENCE. AND
ORGANIZATIONS
MUST INTEGRATE THE
EMOTIONAL NEEDS OF
ALL STAKEHOLDERS,
EMPLOYEES, CUSTOMERS,
AND THE SURROUNDING
COMMUNITY, INTO THEIR
BUSINESS MODEL.

My father was not one of those Leave it to Beaver *fathers. After dinner all the other kids and the fathers would go out and play ball on the streets. My father would finish dinner and go upstairs to where he had his second studio and he would be working. And I was sitting there watching him. And I basically said to him, "Dad, you know I feel badly for you, because all the other fathers come home from work and they get to play with their kids, but you have to go back to work. He put down his brush and he said, "Dean, don't ever feel sorry for me. I love what I do, I am an artist, I get to do something I love all the time. You need to find something that you love to do, and then you'll be the lucky guy."*

Your time on earth is too short to give most of it to a pursuit without excitement or meaning. That means, as an experienced creative, you must serve your emotional needs within your everyday existence. Integration, or an integrated life, is the idea that all aspects of who you are—your home, your work, your community, and your mind/body—are merged into one harmonious state, making you your best self every day.

Practically, this means your life can't be compartmentalized. You mustn't make one-sided decisions. Instead, your decisions and actions must serve all your priorities, all the parts of what makes you who you are. For example, you can't work late at the expense of your relationship with your family. You can only work late if it serves your relationship with your family by making you a more fulfilled individual. You may end up doing many of the same things, but the holistic impact of your actions matters. When you intend to achieve the unbelievable and sustain a fulfilling existence, you can't have fun on Saturdays and be miserable on Mondays; you can't flourish financially but have miserable employees. All aspects of your existence must be served, and all elements must be integrated.

We're all artists, and artists aren't only artists on the weekends; they're artists all the time. You wouldn't stop Picasso or Dali to say it's eight p.m., time to turn off the art and go home. Being an artist, an experienced creative, means you're in touch with your inner purpose, and you don't put it away. Whether parenting, working, making dinner, or sharing your art, you must be like an artist and serve your inner purpose. When you aren't sharing yourself in some meaningful way, you end up cheating yourself and diluting your work. As bestselling author Dr. Brené Brown puts it, "Authenticity is the daily practice of letting go of who we think we're supposed to be and embracing who we are." Your highest art can only be manifested when you achieve integration, when you can always exist as your best self.

For example, when someone cheats in a relationship, most of the time they aren't taking that action because they're a bad person; they do it because they're not getting something they need from within that relationship. Once a persistent "lack" manifests, the individual looks to satisfy that need elsewhere. That's a function of the internal self. The same problem applies in all situations: if you don't serve your internal need to manifest your greater purpose, it will continue to attempt to find its way out. It's what we do as humans; it's innate. Achieving integration—a life that serves all the aspects of who you are or an organization that serves all its stakeholders—creates a positive force in the world and a fertile breeding ground for happiness, fulfillment, and realization of your definition of success.

Imagine that: being in your zone, in your flow, enjoying all your daily experiences fully and being in complete harmony with your environment. Dean Kamen's father wasn't working; he was playing. By living a life that served his purpose, he existed beautifully, carried by the wave of his life.

Integrating Exercise #1: Aligning the 3 P's

Do the following simple exercise to assess the level of integration in your life. It's called aligning your 3 P's: purpose, priority, and position.

Purpose: The reason for which something exists. As we've discussed, it is the WHY behind everything you do, what drives you, what makes you different. It's your essence.

Priority: The relative importance an individual or organization places on various tasks and activities, both short and long term.

Position: What an individual or organization spends every day doing, whether selling carpets or playing soccer.

On a piece of paper, write out your purpose, and then, in one column, write down how you spend your time, e.g., work/school; home/family; community/friends; and body/mind/spirit. (If you're doing this for a business, use the organizational aspects.) Next to each one, assign a percentage out of 100, based on the amount of time they occupy in your life. For example, 30 percent work, 45 percent home, 10 percent community, and 15 percent mind/body. Then, in the adjacent column, assign a 1-5 priority of importance. For example: 1) family, 2) work 3) friends 4) health 5) writing.

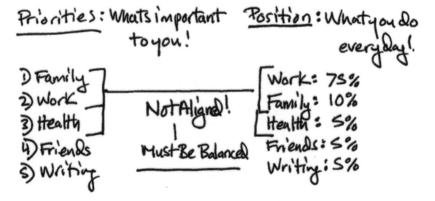

Take a step back and look at the chart. The closer you are to spending the majority of your time on your highest priorities, the closer you are to being aligned and achieving an integration.

Does what you do every day align with the things you claim are most important to you? Are they aligned with your purpose? If not, don't get down on yourself; achieving harmony is a lifelong process. The idea is to understand what you're trying to manifest and then take steps every day to get closer to that goal. When you realize this goal, your internal and external worlds become one, providing you greater strength than you could ever imagine.

The Power of Integration

I think Dean Kamen summarizes the desired result of integration quite well:

"I tell every kid I meet, figure out something you really love to do. Get so good at it that you can make a living doing it. If you don't do that, you're cheating yourself out of a happy, meaningful life." In other words, do what you love, find a way to make money doing it, and positively impact others so it gives your life meaning. Sounds simple, doesn't it? It is. Don't waste your life: learn who you are and what makes you special, and then integrate the things you care about into a meaningful and fulfilling existence.

Choosing Your Challenge

Creator's Formula: Experienced Creativity & Flawless Execution

Follow your bliss and the universe will open doors where there were only walls.

—Joseph Campbell, author, *The Hero with a Thousand Faces*

We are part of a universal cycle of birth, transformation, and death. This cycle is repeated metaphorically throughout our lives, over and over again. You take on a challenge, you transform through some ordeal, your previous existence dies, and you're reborn in some altered form: birth, transformation, death, rebirth. This is what life is all about—trials, tribulations, triumphs, and ongoing transformations. From child to adult, from single to married, from married to parent, from amateur to professional, from employee to entrepreneur, from Anakin Skywalker to Darth Vader, it goes on and on and on.

To be a hero—someone who gives your life to something bigger than yourself, whether it be in your own mind or the minds of others—you must take on challenges. The goal of these challenges is to create and then share your creations for the benefit of something larger than yourself. This is part of our DNA, whether it be manifesting our own journey or engaging with someone else's. It's why we're so enthralled with the achievements of others, whether they be sports stars, entrepreneurs, or just children playing a new song on the piano. It's what we do, it's what we want to do, and it's what makes us feel most fulfilled.

The problem is that most of us don't have a framework to approach our hero's journey, to choose our challenge. And we're principally concerned with our selfish desires, not understanding that our success and fulfillment are wholly dependent on serving a larger purpose.

Successful individuals and organizations not only have a deeper connection to their purpose, they manifest frequently and regularly, giving them many more opportunities to realize their potential. As author Adam Grant points out in his book *Originals*, "Creative geniuses weren't qualitatively better in their fields than their peers. They simply produced a greater volume of work, which gave them more variation and a higher chance of originality." Not every act of creation is going to lead to success, but the likelihood of you creating something truly special increases exponentially the more you create. That is how you become creatively experienced.

What this means is that you must consistently be choosing challenges, a routine you repeat throughout your life, in which you identify the best possible challenge available at any given moment and work to overcome that challenge. After all, as world-class chef Ferran Adrià says, "That is what life is, a struggle to reach a challenge." This idea is at the core of who we are. Why do we play games or sports? They're challenging, and we want to win or go on to the next level. Why do we gamble? It's a never-ending challenge that stimulates us. As humans, these challenges are what give us meaning; they're what we enjoy. Our broader life is no different. Why do you pursue a mate? It's a challenge, and it feels spectacular when you overcome that challenge. The problem is, most of us don't realize that's when the real challenge begins.

But challenges can also be our undoing. When we pursue the wrong challenge—one not aligned with our purpose and not building on our experience—we become unbalanced, and we won't be able to unlock our potential. And that's exactly what we're pursuing: sustainable creative output, the key to true and lasting fulfillment. That means great decision-making is a crucial part of unlocking your potential.

Decisions, Decisions, Decisions

Creator's Formula: Flawless Execution

> *When your values are clear to you, making decisions becomes easier.*
>
> —Roy Disney, cofounder, Walt Disney Productions

A life is made up of the compounded effects of thousands of decisions. The better you get at making those decisions, the higher the likelihood that you'll manifest the existence you desire. The problem is, as a society we're plagued by bad decision-making. Why? Because most individuals and organizations aren't self-aware and lack a framework for making decisions. This combination of not knowing how and not knowing why diminishes the likelihood that you will unlock your creative potential. To become an experienced creative and execute flawlessly you must learn how to identify your highest and best challenge and make better decisions.

At any given moment, there's always a best choice, a best course of action based on your priorities and what you want to achieve. When you're young, these highest and best challenges are quite simple to identify. Say, for example, you're playing with your friends. You can play basketball, soccer, or video games. You like basketball better than soccer and your mom wants you to play outside, so no video games. Clearly, basketball is the highest and best challenge at that moment. As you get older, you want to join a sports team. You want to play basketball, but you're much better at soccer. Now you have to choose what you like to do versus what you have a better chance of succeeding at. On top of that, one of your best friends is playing basketball, the other soccer. Making the best decision just got a lot more complicated.

Life continues on this type of path. Based on our cognitive abilities and the minimal impact of poor decisions, things remain somewhat simple through our early twenties. For the most part, you can make a mistake and recover while still having a high probability of achieving your goals. But once you add spouses, children, aging parents, career demands, and financial planning, the impact of poor decision-making is amplified tenfold. The difference between

A LIFE IS MADE UP OF
THE COMPOUNDED
EFFECTS OF THOUSANDS
OF DECISIONS. THE
BETTER YOU GET
AT MAKING THOSE
DECISIONS, THE HIGHER
THE LIKELIHOOD THAT
YOU'LL MANIFEST THE
EXISTENCE YOU DESIRE.

amazing achievement and complete chaos becomes a couple of poor decisions. Your entire life can change quickly.

And the exact same theory applies to businesses. When you start, the decisions are easy, but the more money and people get involved, the more complicated it gets. That's why going public is such a tough decision; you can reap untold financial gains, but you also end up needing to involve thousands if not millions of share-holders in your decision-making process.

Let's look at the beginning of your career. When you're just starting out, you say yes to almost every challenge. You're just happy to be involved. Whatever opening comes to you, at least you're part of something and learning. But as you grow, you begin to understand who you are, what makes you special, and what you believe you want to do. Immediately, that begins to add filters to the decision-making process; e.g., you want to be a lawyer, so you don't have time to take part-time catering jobs anymore. Simply put, the more you grow, the more you need to say no. At first maybe it's 5 percent of the time: No, I don't want to be in finance, I want to be in the arts. Then it's 10 or 20 percent: No, that's not enough money; or I want a better title or more freedom. But eventually, when you become an experienced creative, it should get to 80, 90, or in some cases 100 percent of the time. When you get to that point, it means you've really begun to understand who you are and what's important to you.

But saying no isn't easy, especially for individuals and organi-zations who love to create. After all, it's difficult to forget there was a time when nobody was asking. And that's a trap, because if you don't say no—if you don't start to filter projects—the work will begin to suffer and you'll slide back on the scale. You'll receive fewer offers and need to say yes more, often taking on projects that draw you further away from your purpose.

Disciplined decision-making is critical. That's why this book offers a framework to help you define your highest and best chal-lenge, guiding you to make choices that meet your short-term needs while bringing you closer to manifesting your purpose and maximizing your long-term return on investment. To discover your highest and best challenge at any given moment, you must look at three factors: purpose/core values, short-term needs, and long-term return on investment. Here's a quick look at each:

Primary Decision Point

- **Purpose:** The first and most important question to ask when making a decision is: Does this opportunity align with my purpose? When you're focused on unlocking your creative potential, your purpose is always your primary decision point; the more closely aligned you are with your purpose, the more likely you'll create work that's unbelievable instead of just ordinary. Are you further integrating what you do every day (your position) and what you desire internally (your purpose)? The more integration of those elements, the better the decision.

Secondary Decision Point

- **Short-Term Needs:** Safety. Security. Shelter. Food. Water. Love. Tuition. Or, for some people, daily vanilla lattes, a weekly night out with their wife, an annual family vacation. While you're working toward unlocking your potential, it's vital that you put yourself in a position to meet your basic short-term needs. Each of us has a different idea of what we need to function effectively, and being brutally honest with yourself about those needs is critical. While anything worth pursuing requires some level of sacrifice, and most of us need less than we think, the secondary factor in determining your highest and best opportunity is to look honestly at whether you'll be able to meet these basic short-term needs when you make this decision.

Tertiary Decision Point

- **Long-Term Returns:** Every time you make a short-term decision, you sacrifice something in the long term, and every time you make a long-term decision, you sacrifice something in the short term. I know that seems obvious, but you'd be surprised at how understanding short term versus long term with this type of perspective provides you a deep level of clarity. When it comes to unlocking your creative potential, you always want to maximize the long-term benefits of your decisions.

For a simple example, let's think about eating cake while on a diet. If you continue to enjoy cake while trying to lose weight, this might satisfy you in the short term but will negatively impact your long-term health and goals. Say no to cake and your short-term satisfaction will suffer, but your long-term health and satisfaction will rise. Conclusion: your long-term returns are greater from not eating that slice of cake. Now, I have nothing against cake; I happen to love it and have made the short-term cake decision countless times. But life is about putting yourself in the position to make more decisions that benefit you in the long term than the short.

There is a famous Stanford University experiment that measured the impacts of being able to delay gratification. Professor Walter Mischel performed these experiments and continued to follow up with his subjects for decades. In the studies, a child was given a choice between one marshmallow provided immediately or two marshmallows if they waited for fifteen minutes. The kids that delayed gratification and waited to receive the second marshmallow ended up having higher SAT scores, lower incidence of substance abuse, lower levels of obesity, better responses to stress, better social skills as reported by their parents, and generally better scores in a range of other life measures. Your ability to make decisions focused on the long term is directly connected to your ability to realize your potential.

Now let me clarify what I mean by returns, because most people will immediately think returns mean money. While you can measure your returns in money, people measure their success differently based on their priorities. Some may seek critical acclaim or to have an impact on others' lives, and some may desire freedom or time spent with their family. It's important to note that only you can define for yourself what you value, and then try to maximize those returns long-term to make the most impact over time.

Challenges = Opportunity
Creator's Formula: Experienced Creativity & Flawless Execution

Going through all this adversity, going through all this difficulty, is what defines you. I'm just thankful to be cooking.
— Chef Danny Bowien

It was October, 2013, and Danny Bowien had just received word that his Manhattan restaurant, Mission Chinese, had been shut down by the health department for an array of violations, including an infestation of mice. Overwhelmed, embarrassed, and worried about his employees, Bowien, a rock-star rising chef, didn't know what to do. It was then that his phone rang. René Redzepi, the chef behind the world's best restaurant, Copenhagen's Noma, and Danny's close friend, said, "Chef, are you ready? They're coming for you. They smell blood. You're hurt, you're wounded and they're going to come for you."

But those weren't Bowien's only worries. At the same time, he was in the midst of opening the Lower East Side taqueria Mission Cantina. The health department issues distracted him, and he canceled a crucial research trip to Mexico. He opened Cantina before it was ready, and the reviews weren't good. Even Redzepi sent him an email saying his tortillas needed an upgrade. After a stretch of being celebrated by peers and customers alike, the once-rising chef was faltering.

Redzepi coached Bowien through his challenges, telling him, "Everything's going to be okay, but you're going to need to handle this. You're going to be fine, but you just need to focus." This encouragement, combined with tough love from another close friend, chef David Chang, founder of Momofuku, spurred Bowien into action. Despite resolving his issues with the health department, Bowien shuttered the original Mission Chinese and set out to start over in a newer, better location.

Bowien came to terms with his adversity and the realization that it had been his own fault. "I got swept up in the whole thing," he remembers. "Doing events everywhere, getting flown all over the world, not being in the restaurants enough. At the end of the day, my time is best spent in the restaurants. This is what got me here." He retrenched, focused, went back to giving the kitchen the benefit of his considerable energy. He gave up alcohol, once his regular companion. The challenges that once could have destroyed him instead were compelling him to rebuild; a stronger, better Danny Bowien would make a stronger, better Mission Chinese.

After a year-plus of hard work, Bowien reopened Mission Chinese in 2014. The original restaurant had sported a beer keg on the floor and was thrown together and cramped. His new location was more civilized, maintaining the edgy, creative energy people expected from him, but through a more refined expression and ambience. The reinvented Mission Chinese is like an artist's work later in his career—self-assured and polished. He's now spending long hours in the kitchen when he's not with his family, focused on his craft and his fatherhood, not his fame. Danny had become an experienced creative. And it shows in the results: the new Mission has snagged three stars from *New York* magazine, two stars from the *New York Times*, and is consistently ranked as one of the best restaurants in arguably the top restaurant city in the world. Just as important, the reborn Mission Chinese is flourishing, with more business than it can handle.

Danny Bowien transformed his challenge into an opportunity.

There are different types of challenges—the ones you choose and the ones that choose you. The key is to embrace them both with the same fervor and positivity. Most of us have similar reactions as those experienced by Danny Bowien when we encounter a challenge we perceive to be negative: panic, anxiety, fear. Thoughts of bad outcomes—worst-case scenarios—become overwhelming and paralyze us. Robert Downey Jr. explained it best when he said, "Worrying is like praying for what you don't want to happen."

But you can shift your perspective and realize that the word *possibilities* inherently means multiple outcomes are in play, both good and bad. Remind yourself that challenges are just as likely to become opportunities or gifts. Whether they're one or the other is greatly determined by your perspective and approach. If you zig when everyone else zags, remaining positive and proactive while others panic, challenges quickly transform into opportunities to rise.

A self-fulfilling prophecy occurs when a person or organization

WORRYING IS LIKE
PRAYING FOR
WHAT YOU DON'T
WANT TO HAPPEN.

unknowingly causes a negative prediction to come true because they expect it to. By making self-fulfilling prophecies positive, you use the power of affirmative thought as a tool to continuously positively impact your reality.

Understanding Your Biases

Creator's Formula: Flawless Execution

> *People only see what they are prepared to see.*
>
> —Ralph Waldo Emerson

Navigation systems such as Google Maps and Waze have changed our lives. No matter where you are in the world, if you have cell phone service, you can figure out how to get where you're going and avoid obstacles on the way. While the reliability and accuracy of these services increases daily through machine-learning and mapping, so too does a condition known as navigation delusion, which occurs when an individual chooses to use their navigation, starts driving, and then willingly does the exact opposite of what the system recommends. I regularly watch in dismay as many of my most-respected friends, family, and business associates openly disagree with their navigation systems. For some reason, they believe their directional knowledge and instincts are superior to a machine designed specifically for that purpose. This isn't one of those situations where human ingenuity surpasses the ability of the computer, and as expected, the results are the same 99.9 percent of the time: traffic gets worse, they arrive late, and they end up saying, "Why didn't I just listen to the navigation?"

And what happens next time? They do the same thing all over again.

This is a perfect example of biased decision-making preventing flawless execution. We're constantly rationalizing, convincing ourselves to do things that aren't in our best interests. It's a flaw in our operating system, an impactful, unconscious form of self-sabotage. I get irritated when someone chooses to disagree with the navigation not because of the delayed arrival but because they knew the path with the highest likelihood of success, of flawless execution, and still chose a different road because of their bias.

Biases are defined as natural inclinations or prejudices for or against people and things. We all have them, and they affect all the decisions we make.

For example, you're interviewing two candidates to join your team. One of them is less qualified but more personable. The other is more qualified but less personable. You consider both candidates, and despite knowing the more qualified one will do a better job, you choose the more personable one. In this case, your biases led you to make a worse decision. It's well documented that most people hire the person who's more personable over the one who's more qualified. And that's exactly the reason you need to understand your biases. Most people don't, and it leads them to make bad decisions, decisions that don't unlock their potential. But if you understand your biases, you'll be one step closer to making decisions that enable flawless execution.

Let's say in the beginning of your career you started a business that failed. That failure led to financial struggles and some real emotional trauma. A couple of years later, after you've recovered, you're offered another entrepreneurial opportunity. You're super-excited, get the investment together, and decide to move forward. Then, as you're reviewing the contracts, fear sets in. You begin to panic, thinking of all the things that could go wrong. Now you don't know if what you're doing is correct. The deal is good, you want to move forward, but you're afraid. Is that fear real? Yes. Is it healthy? Yes. Should you base your decision on it? No. As author and tech-marketing expert Seth Godin says, "Being aware of your fear is smart. Overcoming it is the mark of a successful person." That fear is a bias in your head; it was born of your previous trauma, and you need to recognize that while it's an evolutionary trait—there to protect you—functionally, it has no relevance to your likelihood of success in this situation. You must make decisions based on the facts, not your personal biases.

But how?

Patterns and Handicapping

Creator's Formula: Flawless Execution

While there's no perfect way to recognize your biases, the best way to start is by analyzing the patterns in your life or business. Look

BEING AWARE
OF YOUR FEAR
IS SMART.
OVERCOMING IT
IS THE MARK OF
A SUCCESSFUL
PERSON.

at your business history—if, for example, you notice that during the last two economic downturns, your business struggled more than your competitive set, that could mean you're biased toward taking on too much risk, or potentially that you're making decisions driven more by ego than good business sense. Clearly not flawless execution. If you continue making those types of choices, the odds are you'll end up negatively impacting yourself both personally and professionally. If you recognize and change this pattern, you'll almost certainly improve your results. Recognizing patterns will improve your likelihood of success.

A couple of years ago I joined a football pool with some of my closest friends. While I knew much less than them about football, I joined for the camaraderie. That feeling lasted until I heard the buy-in for the pool was $2,500 per team. The site we were using to manage the league had an advertisement for a guy named Dr. Bob, who claimed to win 51 percent of the time. I looked at the league history and realized no one had ever cracked 45 percent. So I decided I'd buy his picks for the season and use them as my own. I had limited football knowledge, which meant I had no real personal bias for or against his selections. That gave me a real advantage over my highly biased friends, the "experts." And it paid off. Following his picks instead of my own led me to share the winning pot three seasons in a row.

I promise you, non-biased decision-making pays off in the long term.

We all have these types of patterns in our lives—repeated actions that hold us back from achieving the results we desire. Most often they're the result of experiences we (or our organization) went through at an early age and formed our outlook, opinions, and habits. While these factors made us who we are, the goal is to accentuate positive habits and diminish negative ones. Basically, you need to handicap yourself. For our purposes, that means understanding your own level of skill and then diminishing any negative attributes or biases by recognizing them and maintaining vigilant self-awareness to help you succeed.

Think of yourself as Michael Jordan in the second half of his career. As a young player, Michael's physical attributes—specifically, his ability to jump and his quickness—made him nearly impossible to guard. Michael could get to the rim whenever he liked. Later in his career, his physical dominance diminished; therefore, he had to rely more on his jump shot, defensive skills, and knowledge of the game. While his competitive fire never waned, he needed to handicap himself by accepting brutal facts and adjusting his game. The how behind his flawless execution evolved. I'm sure Michael recognized a pattern at some point; maybe he was being stopped more going to the basket or his body couldn't handle the physical impact any longer. Whatever it was, he needed to find another way to execute. He did, and that's one of the many reasons he's the greatest of all time, not just another good player.

Dispassionate Evaluation
Creator's Formula: Flawless Execution

> *The one thing you can't take away from me is the way I choose to respond to what you do to me. The last of one's freedoms is to choose one's attitude in any given circumstance.*
>
> —Viktor Frankl

Viktor Frankl was born to a Jewish family in Vienna, Austria, in 1905. From an early age, he was fascinated with psychology, which led him to study psychiatry and neurology alongside famed psychiatrists Sigmund Freud and Alfred Adler. His studies were centered on suicide and depression. In 1928, he organized a program to counsel high school students, and in 1931, for the first time in years, no high school student committed suicide in Vienna. This accomplishment got him an invitation to Berlin, where he oversaw the suicide-wing of the Steinhof Psychiatric Hospital, treating thousands of patients with suicidal tendencies. In 1938, he was prohibited from treating "Aryan" patients due to his Jewish heritage, so he started overseeing neurology at the Rothschild Hospital, the only facility to which Jews were still admitted.

In 1942, Frankl, his parents, his wife, and his brother were arrested and sent to the Thereisienstadt concentration camp. During the next three years, Frankl experienced four concentration camps, including Auschwitz. He continued to practice psychiatry in the camps, making efforts to address the hopelessness of his fellow inmates. In 1945, Frankl was liberated and returned to Vienna, where he was informed that his entire family had been lost except his sister.

Despite his grief, he returned to his work, using his experiences and observations from the camps to develop a new approach to psychological healing. Frankl named his method logotherapy, founded on the belief that, "It is the striving to find a meaning in one's life that is the primary, most powerful motivating and driving force in humans." He documented his insights in a book, *Man's Search for Meaning*, which went on to sell millions of copies around the world.

Central to Frankl's theories was this concept: "Everything can be taken from a man but one thing; the last of the human freedoms—to choose one's attitude in any given set of circumstances, to choose one's own way." This first-principle truth lies at the essence of what it takes to unlock your creative potential in the world today. Let me attempt to simplify:

Your life is a series of situations, good and bad.

You aren't defined by these situations; you're defined by how you *respond* to these situations.

A life, a career, a relationship is the compounded result of your responses over a period of time.

Think of it as a scorecard, with little boxes monitoring your responses: good, okay, and bad. Your goal is to maximize the positive responses and minimize the negative ones.

As Frankl said, "Between stimulus and response there is a space. In that space is our power to choose our response. In our response lies our growth and our freedom."

In your response you have the ability to define yourself, to allow your best self to shine through. The best tool to enable yourself to do that is *dispassionate evaluation*—to take that moment between stimulus and response to step back, analyze the situation without emotion, and to flawlessly execute without letting negative emotional biases affect your judgment.

In all scenarios, both personal and business, the party that controls its emotions and biases rises.

The idea of dispassionate evaluation may sound counterintuitive, since this book is about valuing emotion as a tool to help you connect with your purpose and share that purpose with others, but

YOUR LIFE IS A SERIES
OF SITUATIONS,
GOOD AND BAD. YOU
AREN'T DEFINED BY
THESE SITUATIONS;
YOU'RE DEFINED BY
HOW YOU RESPOND
TO THESE SITUATIONS.
A LIFE, A CAREER, A
RELATIONSHIP IS THE
COMPOUNDED RESULT
OF YOUR RESPONSES
OVER A PERIOD OF TIME.

it's important to understand that emotion can impair our ability to flawlessly execute. Dispassionate evaluation requires that you look at the situation objectively, eliminating feelings related to your biases, so that you can clearly assess the practical positive and negative impacts of that decision.

For example, let's say you have an opportunity to make a movie you've been working hard on for two years. There's a deal with a big studio to make the movie, and it will involve that studio giving you lots of feedback and guidance on the artistic direction of the film. You immediately react negatively to the idea that they're going to have a strong say in how your movie is made. You fear your voice is going to be lost in the process, and you are angry and frustrated. But...this is your best chance to get the movie made, it will lead to incredible career growth, and it will further your opportunities in the filmmaking field. At this point you need to take a step back, breathe deeply, and make a dispassionate evaluation. Is the executive in charge known for being difficult and intrusive, or patient and helpful? Are there other studios likely to step up as well, or is this your only option? Do you have an advocate at the studio with enough clout to help you protect the project? If the film ends up being poorly received, will it prevent you from getting more movies made, or will the credit outweigh any negativity around the film?

While you may have concerns that can push this decision in one direction or another, the bias here lies with your ego and desire for control. If you put aside your fear and other emotions, you will be able to assess the opportunity realistically. It may become clear that moving forward, whatever the challenges, is worth the risk. In this simplified scenario, your potential career growth outweighs your short-term loss of control. But if you allow the negative emotions to drive the process and make a passionate evaluation, you'll likely end up making the wrong decision—or even if it's the right decision, you'll be less prepared to manage the difficulties when they do arise.

Let's look at one more example. You work in sales. For over a year you've been working on a deal that's days from closing. You need the sale to happen to reach your quota and achieve your bonus. The client comes back and completely changes a key term. You are furious; after a year of working on this deal, how could your counterpart even suggest something so egregious and insulting? So what do you do? Well, you could blow up the deal, tell your counterpart to f*ck off and go to hell. What would be the result of that? Complete negativity. The end of the deal, the end of the relationship, no commission for you, and a missed quota. Or you could take a deep breath, remove your emotions from the situation, perform a dispassionate evaluation, and calmly and strongly respond to your counterpart that the change isn't reasonable, especially at such a late stage in your dealings. You ask what their concern is and look for a way to address it without conceding to something onerous or walking away in anger. In this scenario, you're leaving all options open for the deal, yourself, and your financial well-being. If they want the deal, it will happen in some form; if not, you gave it the best chance to happen and can walk away without regret (at least about your own actions).

Dispassionate evaluation is a four-step process:

Step One: *Pause, take a deep breath, and think. I highly recommend meditation or yoga, but quiet contemplation works as well.*

Step Two: *Recognize which negative emotions and biases are present, then remove them from the decision-making process. Acknowledge them and set them to the side.*

Step Three: *Perform an analysis of the situation that focuses on how each potential decision will impact the desired long-term results for all key stakeholders.*

Step Four: *Move forward with positivity, generosity, and respect for all parties involved.*

This simple four-step tool may be the most valuable part of this book. By performing this simple analysis, you can remove the most prevalent negative aspects of your personality and amplify your most positive traits. The result is a supercharging of your ability to reach goals thanks to the compound effects of good decision-making, the foundation of flawless execution.

Mentors, Coaches, and Trusted Advisors
Creator's Formula: Flawless Execution

Show me a successful individual and I'll show you someone who had real positive influences in his or her life. I don't care what you do for a living—if you do it well I'm sure there was someone cheering you on or showing the way. A mentor.

—Denzel Washington

You may have noticed a number of the life stories we've been discussing have featured mentors and advisors sharing wisdom, pointing the way. Rick Rubin's role as a music producer certainly involved advising and coaching as he worked with artists to manifest their creativity. Danny Bowien, in his time of crisis, was helped by the insights of his friends and fellow chefs René Redzepi and David Chang. Michael Bonadies and Harry Bernstein mentored me. Harry had his own mentors. Even Michael Jordan, and another world-class athlete we'll encounter soon, New England Patriots quarterback Tom Brady, were aided by two of the greatest sports coaches in history: Phil Jackson and Bill Belichick, respectively.

And one of the great gifts a mentor, advisor, or coach can bestow on a person trying to make the most of their talents is enhanced self-awareness.

Being self-aware is having a conscious knowledge of one's character, feelings, motives, and desires. While many of us fancy ourselves self-aware, the truth is that most of us are not. And no matter how many exercises, therapist appointments, and meditation sessions we partake in, we probably will never be as self-aware as we would like. This is because we are inexorably blinded by our ego and internal monologue.

We see only what we want to see.

The surest way to consistently and effectively neuter the destructive power of your ego is to have a mentor, coach, or community of trusted advisors who can provide you honest, non-biased feedback and guidance. These people are the real mirrors of your behavior, the ones giving you the truth that a standard mirror cannot. For example, how many times have you looked in the mirror and thought, *I don't look good, I look fat, my hair is not right*. Newsflash—this has nothing to do with reality. It has everything to do with your internal monologue. When and if you quiz a good friend, life partner, or parent about your observation, inevitably they respond, "What are you talking about, you look great," or "Change your pants, red is not your color." The same applies to finding the right job or managing a conflict with your coworker or spouse. The point is a trusted advisor provides invaluable dialogue and grounded feedback that helps calm your inner monologue, enhances your understanding of the truth of who you are or how you are acting, and gives you the tools to manifest your best self.

To honestly see ourselves we must be able to look through the eyes of another and trust what they see. Flawless execution is simply not possible without this type of feedback.

While many of us have experienced the benefits of a positive individual in our lives, more often than not it is by accident. You ended up in a high school class with a teacher who cared a little more. Or you had an aunt who really took the time to nurture your love of music. Or you had a great boss who helped you grow as a manager. Without a doubt these types of relationships help you flourish, but I believe we need to flip the engagement of mentors from passive to active. The counsel, feedback, and support of the "right" person is so crucial to raising the level of your execution that leaving it to chance is unwise.

Your full potential will not be realized without the assistance of a series of mentors, coaches, and trusted advisors. You must actively pursue and nurture these relationships.

While approaching potential mentors may sound nerve-wracking, I promise you'll be gratified by how people respond to your requests. First off, most people are flattered when someone asks for their counsel because inherently it means they have achieved a level of status. Secondly, whether they realize it or not, you are giving them the greatest gift imaginable. There is no better path to fulfillment than being able to help another. So if they respond positively, the mentor will probably end up getting more out of the relationship than the mentee, and if they respond negatively, they are probably not at the level of consciousness you want in a mentor.

There is no harm in asking and I guarantee more often than not you will be happy with the response.

The realization of your best self and your best work will involve dozens of people. Of those individuals that nurture your talents, provide opportunities, or just give you sage advice, there will be a handful that unselfishly invest their time and energy in you. Find these people and hold on to them with all your might. They will be invaluable to your process—and more importantly, to your life. The right mentor will help you do what you can, be who you are, and open you to the endless possibilities that lie within. And if you're lucky, one day you will be able to do the same for another.

Grasping and implementing these tools will lead you to understand yourself at a deeper level and bring you closer to the flawless execution of your ideas. This is a vital step in unlocking your capabilities; when you choose the right opportunities, they bring you closer to your ultimate goal. Combine this with the compounding nature of decisions, both good and bad, and the impact of your decisions are amplified considerably. Self-sustaining positive-energy loops naturally exist in the world, and these tools allow you to ride them like a surfer on a wave.

Building Your Wave

Creator's Formula: Experienced Creativity & Flawless Execution

> *I was 18 when I first started working at a restaurant. I was a dishwasher. I only got the job because I wanted to go to Ibiza for vacation, and washing dishes was the only job I could find.*
>
> —Chef Ferran Adrià

When I was a young man I wanted to be a chef. Food always fascinated me. I loved to taste it, I loved to cook it, and I loved—well, before the rise of food porn, I loved to read about food, talk about food, and watch people prepare it. When other kids were watching *The Price Is Right* on days home sick from school, I watched *The Frugal Gourmet*, *Yan Can Cook*, and shows featuring Julia Child, TV's cooking matriarch. Combine this passion with an over-encouraging mother and an Italian grandmother who made a mean Sunday gravy, and you have all the makings of a future chef.

I followed my passion diligently, even at a young age, constantly experimenting and honing my craft. Then, opportunity knocked: close friends of my mother were friendly with Wolfgang Puck (thank you, Ron and Nancy), and encouraged me to write to him to apply for a culinary stage my junior year of high school. I followed her advice, and a few months later, during summer break, I headed to Los Angeles to work in the kitchen at Wolfgang's original restaurant, Spago, on the Sunset Strip. After a couple of bumps in the road (including not knowing that chefs brought their own knives to work), I hit my stride and began the daily grind that is working in a professional kitchen.

The backbone of modern kitchens is formed by immigrants (many illegal), who are highly skilled cooks but willing to work for the wages that give restaurants the possibility of making a profit, and young culinary students willing to work for next to nothing to learn their craft. I spent months chopping fruits, vegetables, herbs, and spices, occasionally worked on meats or fish, and, when I was lucky, got to prepare a staff meal. The experience was magical. I still remember the smells, the tastes, and even the first time I ever got drunk—with the staff—and spent the next morning in the bathroom throwing up when I wasn't chopping jalapeños while the staff cheered me on. I rubbed my bloodshot eyes with the same hands I used to chop the jalapeños—and let's just say it was a painful mistake I never made again.

After a couple of months, just as I was getting the hang of it, I had to leave. School was starting, I had a girlfriend back in New York, and it was my senior year of high school. I remember returning and being really stoked about cooking, but I was also no longer in the kitchen. While Wolfgang wrote me a college recommendation and I got accepted to Cornell, I also got back into the regular life of a teenager. And the further I drifted from the energy of that kitchen, the more I convinced myself I would be wasting my talents as a chef. Why should I be a manual laborer when I could use my Ivy League degree to become a wealthy businessman? Most chefs made an hourly wage, and I would probably have to spend many years struggling. So I abandoned my dream and pursued the business side of hospitality. While the decision worked out well for me professionally, I can say without question that not pursuing a career in the kitchen is a decision I continue to regret.

While in general I don't believe in regret, I keep it alive in my consciousness in this case as a reminder that I made a decision for the wrong reasons. I wasn't willing to sacrifice my short-term comfort to pursue the purest form of my purpose. I didn't recognize or accept that I couldn't start at the top; my ego got in the way, as it does for many of us. If Mark Zuckerberg can start Facebook and be the CEO, isn't anything less a failure? After all, that's what the media sells us. We've discussed the error in this kind of thinking, but at the time, I was blissfully unaware of it, and it cost me—maybe not financially, but in many other ways.

Ferran Adrià

Hailed as a genius and a prophet by fellow chefs, worshipped (if often misunderstood) by critics and lay diners alike, imitated and paid homage to in restaurant kitchens all over the world, Ferran Adrià is easily the most influential serious chef of the late twentieth and early twenty-first centuries. Quite simply, he changed the game.

—Colman Andrews, food critic

It wasn't always that way.

Fernando Adrià Acosta, a/k/a Ferran Adrià, was born on May 14, 1962, in a crowded, demographically diverse area southwest of Barcelona. His father, Gines, was a painter and plasterer, and his mother, Josefa, a housewife. He did well in his studies but was also a regular at the local discos. Ferran more or less lived for Thursday nights—there was no school on Fridays, so that was when the long weekend would begin. After three years of upper school, he dropped out.

"If you asked me why," he says, "I couldn't tell you. It was just a decision I made one day." Ferran didn't leave school with a plan; he wanted to play as much soccer as possible and make some money so he could go to Ibiza in the summer. Ferran's father had an old friend named Miquel Moy who was the chef at the Hotel Playafels, a seaside resort. As Gines tells it, "Miquel and I went to a bar to have a beer one day, and I said to him, 'My son has quit school and needs to find a job. Maybe he would like to work at your hotel.'" Miquel mentioned kitchen work. Gines replied, "Miquel, I have to warn you: Fernando doesn't know anything about cooking at all." Just then, Ferran arrived. His father explained that Miquel had agreed to hire him. With nothing else to do, Ferran said, "Okay, let's go."

On Sunday, June 15, 1980—my first birthday, as it happens—Ferran started work in the kitchen. At this point he had to make a decision: soccer or cooking. "They wanted me to work on Sundays, and Sunday was the day we played soccer, so I had to choose between the job and the playing field," said Ferran. Before deciding, he went to his soccer coach to ask for a realistic analysis of his skills. The coach told him the Third Division was probably the best he could hope for, so Ferran decided to put his energy toward his new job. He started as a *fregador*, basically a dishwasher, and he did that for about three months. Eventually, Miquel Moy, a good, classically trained Spanish chef, let him help with the cooking. Moy's bible was *El Práctico*, a collection of 6,500 recipes from Spain, France, and elsewhere, written in 1895 by two Argentinian chefs. He gave a copy to Ferran, and for the next nine months Ferran spent his mornings studying *El Práctico*, his days in the kitchen, and his evenings in the discos. "Under Moy," Ferran remembers, "we could be up until eight a.m. [partying], but an hour later, we had to be in, and shape up to work normally and seriously. The rule was to arrive on time and stay right till the end."

One day, Moy called Gines and said, "Please take your son back, because now this boy knows more than me." Having saved some money, Ferran headed to Ibiza, then ended up back in a kitchen at a resort hotel. He spent four months cooking, partying, and lounging on the beach before heading home. In Barcelona and environs, he did brief culinary stages in multiple places, including a tapas bar inside a bingo parlor; a conference and party venue in a fourteenth-century villa; Martinica, where Ferran had what he calls his first contact with "modern cooking"; and Finisterre, an elegant, old-style restaurant then considered to be among Barcelona's best.

In 1982, Ferran was drafted into Spain's military and posted to a naval base in Cartagena, Colombia. He volunteered for culinary service and spent a month in the barracks kitchen, preparing massive quantities of simple food for the sailors. During his time there, he was scouted by the head butler for the household of the base commander, Admiral Ángel Liberal Lucini. Lucini liked good food, and the butler was his talent scout. After a few culinary tests, such as making mayonnaise, paella, and vichyssoise, Ferran was ranked *bien* and asked to join the admiral's kitchen.

Although he expected it to be a cushy posting, he quickly realized he not only had to think up new menus every day for the admiral's family, but also to conceive and execute serious banquets for visiting dignitaries. It was here, alongside his close friend and future collaborator Fermí Puig, that Ferran began experimenting with new techniques. Puig came armed with an arsenal of books on haute cuisine, and they used them to prepare meals for the admiral and his guests. They prepared everything from salmon terrine with green peppercorns and rich aspic to Loup en Croûte, legendary chef Paul Bocuse's preparation of bass in a pastry shell. The work would eventually result in Ferran's first book, *El Sabor del Mediterráneo*, a combination of the recipes used for the banquets and some "daydreams" Ferran never even prepared.

When it came time for Ferran to take his summer leave from the navy, Puig convinced him to do a stage at the Spanish restaurant he worked in prior to the military, El Bullí. Ferran initially had no interest in spending his vacation in the kitchen. But the combination of two Michelin stars and a beautiful beach eventually got him to relent. Ferran traveled to coastal Roses and spent a month under Chef Jean Paul-Vinay, immersed in haute cuisine. After three weeks, remembers Puig, "[The manager] called to say, 'Hey, Fermí, no offense, but that guy you sent, Fernando, he's much better than you.'"

At the end of 1983, Ferran finished his military service. He spent a few months working in Seville before reuniting with Puig to begin work full time at El Bullí. When Ferran joined the staff, Juli Soler, the manager, encouraged him to travel to expose himself to fresh ideas and cultures. Ferran toured some of France's top kitchens, learning various techniques from culinary greats. He eventually took over as head chef, and at the beginning of 1987, he went to the Côte d'Azur. In Nice, he stayed in the Negresco, whose restaurant, the Chantecler, was run by famed chef Jacques Maximin. He attended a culinary demonstration by Maximin, and during the discussion that followed, the chef was asked what creativity was. Maximin replied, "*Creativity means not copying.*" This simple sentence brought about a crucial change in Ferran's cooking—the cutoff point between his "re-creation" of others' dishes and a firm decision to become deeply involved in his own creativity.

Upon returning to El Bullí, Ferran, then 25, was convinced he needed to use cookbooks less and less and try to find an identity of his own. He gradually began to experiment with new techniques for preparing and presenting food, and by 1994, four years after becoming co-owner of the restaurant, he had moved away from classic approaches altogether. He had become an experienced creative. He replaced conventionality with his own creation, "technique-concept cuisine," today often referred to as "molecular gastronomy," in which he subjected potential ingredients to rigorous experimentation and scientific analysis as a means of creating novel dishes that produced unexpected sensations. The most famous example was his use of "spherification," which delicately encapsulates liquids within spheres of gelatin. One of the best-known examples are his "liquid olives," which resemble solid green olives but burst in the mouth with olive juice.

Almost twenty years after arriving at El Bullí and following tens of thousands of kitchen hours, Ferran Adrià was widely regarded as the world's most creative, if not in fact the premier, living chef. In 2002, El Bullí was named the best restaurant in the world, and went on to receive the honor five times before closing in 2011 to become, fittingly, a creativity-research center. Ferran is hailed as "the Salvador Dali of the kitchen," and his work has been thoroughly documented in more than thirty books, exhibited in museums, and copied (with both good and bad results) all over the globe.

But Ferran's unbelievable achievement didn't come easy.

He built his wave of success meticulously over decades, through a combination of patience, struggle, experimentation, self-awareness, team-building, and silent struggle in a remote restaurant with few customers and limited resources early on. Every success, every experiment, every hour of thought, every piece of advice, every decision he made compounded on the next, eventually creating a self-sustaining energy, a wave, that over time carried him to a peak.

Your pursuit is no different.

Your Wave

Good and evil both increase at compound interest. That is why the little decisions you and I make every day are of such infinite importance. The smallest good act today is the capture of a strategic point from which, a few months later, you may be able to go on to victories you never dreamed of.

— C. S. Lewis

Have you ever sat on the beach and watched the waves? If you have, you will have noticed they start small, build up slowly, peak, and then break as they crash into the shore. The best surfers are able to spot the wave as it's building, set themselves up, enjoy an amazing ride, and seamlessly move onto the next without wiping out.

Creating is no different.

All our waves, our journeys, start small, build up slowly, and, over time, reach a peak; every decision we make, big and small, all the work we do, compounds to make us who we become. Your wave, your ability to flawlessly execute, is the compounding effect of combining good decisions with great execution, repetitively. The more focused we are in our pursuit, the better the decisions we make, the harder we work, the more likely our wave will be significant, the more energy it will have, the more interesting life becomes.

Your Wave = (Good Decisions + Great Execution)

Every part of Ferran's process—the building of his wave—brought him closer to manifesting a reflection of his true self, and when he achieved that reflection his ability to flawlessly execute emerged. But it took years. (Also note what his former student and friend Jose Andres observed: "This guy is at the top of the top. Usually when people are at the top of their game, it's at this moment in life when you are willing to give everything you have. Warren Buffett, Bill Gates. It's great. But one of the things that has made this man

YOUR WAVE

=

Good Decisions

+

Great Execution

unique—and I think sometimes it's a story the press has not been able to tell—is that twenty-five years ago when only maybe a few of us knew him, he was also a giver. And...to give everything when you have nothing, that's even more amazing.")

Once you have the knowledge of how to unlock your creative potential, your ability to manifest that potential, to flawlessly execute, starts small. In the beginning, you're learning, marshaling your resources, forming a point of view, meeting collaborators. At that point you only have the ability to manifest small waves. While you may have big desire, your skills and resources have yet to catch up, so it would be ill-advised for you to take on a project too large. But these simple, focused projects are critical to your long-term success: everything you're learning will be part of the bigger waves you'll build later in your journey. Once you carry out your first small project, you should analyze the outcome and then do another, focusing on improving each time. When you do this over and over again, you'll eventually see your first wave beginning to form. Maybe people at work are talking about how hard you work, or how well you manage the front desk at the hotel, or that one of your dishes got on the menu. It may or may not be the wave you thought it was—maybe an opportunity opens up that wasn't really what you thought you wanted—but that's not important; all that matters is that you're making waves, you're progressing toward your first peak.

These peaks are the moments where you're doing the best work you can on this wave. For example, I started out in food and beverage. I've mentioned that eventually I came to oversee a $150-million food-and-beverage business on multiple continents. It was a fantastic wave. But I knew if I wanted to achieve my long-term goals, I had to get off that wave and start the learning that would build my next wave. Now, for some of us, waves can last decades, even a lifetime; it really all depends on what challenges present themselves and what you desire.

The more focused and skilled you become, the bigger your waves will grow. And then your waves will merge with waves from the surrounding energy of the world and take you on some amazing rides. Ferran's first wave was in Miquel Moy's kitchen. The global press didn't care, but he impressed Miquel, and that was all that mattered. As his skills grew, so did his ability to make waves. His next wave was in the military kitchen. There, his wave was a little bigger and touched more people, each time helping Ferran become a better surfer. His subsequent wave was in El Bullí. That one took over a decade to reach its peak. He needed intense focus, greater skills, and more self-examination to get him closer to his potential. The wave peaked when it merged with two external waves that carried him to new heights: the rise of nouveau Spanish cuisine on the global stage, and the rise of global foodie culture. And finally, that wave peaked after two decades in the kitchen, and like a skilled surfer he saw it breaking and seamlessly moved onto the next stage of his journey.

Too often, people are looking for shortcuts, ways to get to the peak without doing the work. But it's impossible to surf without being able to paddle into the wave—being able to recognize it and have the strength to pull yourself into it and up. Shortcuts are a bullshit way of avoiding the necessary work, and more to the point, they rarely bring sustained success. While you can be strategic in your approach—you shouldn't try to get up on every wave—there's no way to avoid putting in the necessary energy it takes to do great work.

Remember, ideas are just ripples—waves manifest when energy is added to the equation and you flawlessly execute your ideas.

Cultivating Appreciation
Creator's Formula: Emotional Generosity

> *Too often in life, something happens and we blame other people for us not being happy or satisfied or fulfilled.*
> —Tom Brady, quarterback, New England Patriots

Capitalism harnesses our selfish desires to fuel the growth of society. It rightfully assumes that when freedom is combined with desire, individuals will obey their self-interest and work hard to improve their position.

While I'm a rabid capitalist, the system isn't without flaws. When most of our focus is on growth, material goods, and financial returns, it's inevitable that we'll constantly lack fulfillment and emotional generosity. And that lack has powerful negative implications. Our endless desire for more must be counterbalanced by the cultivated appreciation of what we have, for without that appreciation, the personal fulfillment we all seek isn't possible. Just think of the multitude of parents obsessed with their children's future achievements rather than enjoying the pure bliss of their child every day.

This same lack of appreciation is a major barrier for both individuals and organizations looking to manifest their creative potential. Our capitalistic obsession with growth, material goods, and financial returns is in direct opposition to our ability to be emotionally generous and therefore manifest our full potential.

For a simple example of this, look no further than publicly traded companies. These organizations are slaves to growth, because their stock price (and therefore value) is based on future earnings. If they don't hit their quarterly numbers, their stock goes down and the company is worth less. This often leads to companies making short-term decisions like cutting great people or killing development projects to achieve quarterly results. Does that make the company more likely to achieve greatness long term? Absolutely not.

The likelihood of realizing our potential increases tenfold when appreciation is cultivated, when we are emotionally generous. For example, Tom Brady has four Super Bowl rings and a legitimate claim to the title of greatest quarterback to ever play football, but *Forbes* recently called him "the biggest bargain in sports." So what gives? Aren't the two in complete opposition? While I have little concern for Tom's overall financial situation, it's notable that he earns less than almost a dozen other quarterbacks and could easily command significantly more. Why doesn't he? Well, it seems Tom cares more about pursuing his potential—a/k/a winning Super Bowls—than he does his personal financial growth. Or, simply, he balances his selfish desire for more with a cultivated appreciation of what he already has—in this case his teammates. And that emotional generosity, along with one of the greatest coaches in football history, is what makes the New England Patriots perennial favorites to win the Super Bowl.

Lacking appreciation and emotional generosity is endemic to our society and the human condition. It leads us to believe that fulfilling our selfish desires will bring the fulfillment and success we crave. But only when we transcend this impulse and give meaning-

OUR ENDLESS DESIRE FOR MORE MUST BE COUNTERBALANCED BY THE CULTIVATED APPRECIATION OF WHAT WE HAVE, FOR WITHOUT THAT APPRECIATION, THE PERSONAL FULFILLMENT WE ALL SEEK ISN'T POSSIBLE.

fully to others can we truly appreciate our gifts and manifest them to their greatest potential.

Appreciation Exercise #1: The Little Things

Take a moment and close your eyes. Imagine you have nothing.

Your family, friends, favorite shirt, television, dog, iPhone, even your ability to speak, taste, and hear are all gone.

Take a moment to think about the simple things: a hug, a kiss, a smile from someone special, a warm shower, a conversation with someone close to you, a sip of your morning coffee, listening to your favorite song.

How wonderful are each of these small moments?

Now, think of your life today, all the amazing people, things, and moments you enjoy every day. On a pad, list the ten things you are most thankful for. Take this list and tape it up on your bathroom mirror so you can look at it every day when you are brushing your teeth.

Shift your focus from what you don't have to what you do have.

When you experience life through this lens, it's filled with appreciation. And when you cultivate your appreciation, you'll experience magic every day.

The Right People

Creator's Formula: Emotional Generosity

Danny Meyer is the spiritual leader of the hospitality business. Through his restaurants like Shake Shack and Gramercy Tavern, and books like *Setting the Table*, he has achieved incredible financial success and esteem. But Meyer's contribution transcends hospitality. Since opening Union Square Cafe in 1985, he has been transformed into an evangelist of sorts. He preaches and teaches "enlightened hospitality"—the understanding and application of how the delivery of a product makes its recipient feel. Meyer understands that "good service," the technical delivery of a product, has become an expectation; therefore culture and experience have become the true differentiators. As he puts it, "It's all about how you make the customer feel." Sound familiar? That sounds like emotional generosity to me.

The most important step in creating a hospitable culture is hiring the right people. Meyer calls these people "fifty-one per-centers"—team members with a high hospitality quotient, whose skills are 49 percent technical and 51 percent emotional. You can teach someone a technical skill, but it's much more difficult to teach them emotional skills. The core skills Meyer looks for are optimism and kindness, curiosity about learning, an exceptional work ethic, a high degree of empathy, and self-awareness and integrity. As Meyer explains it, "By putting your employees first, you have happier employees, which then leads to a higher HQ. A higher HQ leads to happy customers, which benefits all the stakeholders. The cycle is virtuous, not linear, because the stakeholders all impact each other."

All businesses are dependent on people. That's because great experiences only occur when one person connects with another, when someone is emotionally generous. When the person on the receiving end of the product or service leaves happier and more fulfilled, the transaction was a success. It's precisely this emotional connection that increases positive sentiment and eventually grows into a successful brand or movement.

Doing this once is quite simple. Almost anyone, for example, can throw one really great dinner party. But when you multiply that one interaction by hundreds, thousands, or even millions, that's where the problems begin. How can you possibly make all those connections meaningful and memorable? But organizations like Meyer's Shake Shack manage to do it. Many believe this comes from training, but training is technical. Recruitment—the practice of finding new people to join an organization or support a cause—is truly the most important step in the process. When you empower the right people, emotionally generous people, they will make the right decisions. Or, as Danny Meyer says, "The overarching concern to do the right thing well is something we can't train for. Either it's there or it isn't."

Creating Happiness
Creator's Formula: Emotional Generosity

> *I don't think human beings were made to be worshipped.*
> *We are here to serve each other and that's the only way we*
> *can keep our sanity. People who give back don't go crazy.*
> *And people who just take and take and take and are wor-*
> *shipped and are just receiving, they lose their minds.*
>
> —Scooter Braun

Scooter Braun is a talent manager and entrepreneur. While he is widely known for discovering Justin Bieber, he also manages Kanye West, Ariana Grande, the Black-Eyed Peas, The Knocks, and David Guetta, among many others. Braun started as a party promoter in Atlanta when he was at Emory University. At the time, his goal was to be a billionaire. After about a month of being in business, he realized that "making five grand was really hard" and that being a billionaire was not reasonable. A day came when he was introduced to a successful older man with a wife, kids, a small boat, a nice home. Braun asked the man how much he would have to earn over the years to enjoy a similar life. After the man offered an "extremely high but reasonable number," Braun told himself, "I am going to work to my fifties or sixties" and reach this figure.

At the time, he was twenty years old.

Seven years later, Scooter Braun called his accountant and asked, "How much cash do I have right now after taxes?" The accountant did some checking and cited a figure already higher than the financial goal Braun had set at age twenty. He called his dad to share the good news, and the elder Braun offered congratulations. Then Scooter said, "But, Dad, here's the problem. I thought when I got here I would be happy."

Thankfully, as Braun put it, his dad gave him the "best advice in the world." He told his son to hang up the phone, think about when he was last genuinely happy, and call him back. Driving at the time, Braun pulled over, thought about it for a while, then got back on the phone with his dad. "Okay, it's going to sound crazy," he began, before sharing times when he last felt genuinely happy:

"Just sitting at night and hanging out with my [kids]; when I am playing ball, get hot on the court and hit a couple of threes in a row; when I go to a children's hospital; when I am answering somebody randomly back on Facebook." His dad's response? The older Braun told his son now he was in a position to achieve *real success*, and went on to describe what this would be: "Success is the freedom to do the things that you actually love. So implement more of those things into your life and you will get happiness. And as you get more money you can implement more and more."

This led Scooter Braun to the following conclusion: "[As] we get older we get in this place where we have to provide. And we got to go to a job every single day and that's why we start to get broken down. Because we are taking more and more time away from what actually makes us happy. And then we get to a place where you made some money, and you're continuing in the rat race, and you're like, What the hell did I do this for? I want people to have the perspective that you can make a lot of money or not make a lot of money, but that doesn't define your happiness. Your choice of balance in your life decides your happiness, your choice of how much you want to give to others, the choice of friends and family you want to spend time with. If you make the conscious decision, [you] can implement more of that in your life right now."

You are here to serve a purpose beyond yourself. To discover what you excel at and enjoy and then apply your energy to help yourself and others live a more fulfilled existence. When you evolve your thoughts, intentions, and actions to discover your true self and apply this philosophy to be emotionally generous, your world will open up in ways you never could have imagined.

PART FOUR: THE RULES OF MAGIC

Our goals can only be reached through the vehicle of a plan, in which we must fervently believe, and upon which we must vigorously act. There is no other route to success.

—Pablo Picasso

Gelareh Mizrahi

The Designer Behind The Coolest Clutches In The World.
—*Nylon* magazine headline

I knew she was different when I met her. She was petite, around five feet tall and ninety pounds, with big eyes and a captivating smile that implied, "I know something you don't, and I am not going to tell you what it is." But beyond her beauty, she was extraordinarily creative, with the kind of energy that bubbles up without intention—it's just part of who she is. When you combine that type of creative energy with sensitivity, kindness, and a love of family, you're talking about my ideal woman...which is why I asked her to be my wife. But it just so happens that Gelareh Mizrahi is also a perfect example of what everyone can manifest in the Age of Ideas.

When I met her, Gelareh had recently graduated from the Parsons School of Design and was helping her cousin Aimee with her clothing brand, Queen of e.vil. The two of them would lock themselves in Aimee's apartment for endless hours and cook up crazy design ideas that would end up on T-shirts, sweatshirts, and cashmere sweaters sold in department stores and boutiques from Dallas to Dubai. (You know that amazingly inspirational gear you pick up at SoulCycle? Aimee and Gelareh came up with the initial designs.) But before long, Gelareh, with her creative energy and desire, needed a new outlet; she wanted more.

That was when the universe (and her mother) swooped in.

One afternoon Gelareh's mother Gilda was working in her boutique in Georgetown, an upscale area in Washington D.C. A customer noticed the python-skin handbags she had for sale and commented, "You know, I could make similar handbags for you. Maybe I could do a private label for your store." Gilda said, "I don't really want a private label, but you should speak with my daughter. She's a fashion designer in New York." And so Gelareh was put in touch with this woman, who owned a factory that produced handbags. A couple of conversations and emails later, an arrangement was in place: Gelareh would design and sell the python handbags in the U.S., while the woman would handle producing the bags overseas, and they would see how things developed from there.

I was skeptical; yes, she had a partner, but no start-up capital. Why wouldn't she just get a job doing design for someone else? But Gelareh was determined, and when she is determined, get on board or get out of the way.

The first step for her new business was to get a booth at the Coterie show, a wholesale fashion tradeshow where all the major retailers buy from all the major producers. When you aren't a recognized name, they don't just hand you a booth, and most booths are committed months in advance. If a newcomer is lucky enough to score a space, it's usually way in the back. That's what happened here. Gelareh designed a low-cost but appealing booth for the Coterie show, and her father, brother, and I built it on-site, way in the back of the Jacob Javits convention center.

I wanted to help with the sales process, but Gelareh was not having it. She asked me to go back to work and show up when it was time to break the booth down. Each night she came home exhausted, collapsed in bed, and left the next morning at the break of dawn. When the Coterie show ended, I broke down the booth. As we began our drive home, Gelareh was silent. She had not shared any sales numbers, so I was worried that no sales had been made. I was afraid of the impact this might have on her confidence and our new enterprise. But before long a subtle grin began to show on her face.

I felt inspired to ask, "So did you make any sales?"

"Maybe," she replied.

"How much you take in?"

After a pause, she blurted, "We made $48,000!"

"What?!" I cried. And proceeded to scream with glee like a young girl getting her first Barbie doll.

Now, let's stop for a moment. Gelareh did not own a factory. She did not have a sales force—or *any* employees, for that matter. The business at this point was entirely financed by the bag producer, a lucky break, but the start-up costs were no more than $20,000. Gelareh went from an idea to an international brand in less than a year with no personal capital investment and only the strength of her creative designs.

From there things continued to evolve. As the business grew, Gelareh renamed the company *Gelareh Mizrahi* and used the Internet, mainly Google and Alibaba, to find a new producer who could handle much higher capacity. With full control of her brand, she decided to fully express her creative vision, and her designs became more personal. She combined her love of high fashion with her Persian heritage and her experiences roaming the streets of D.C. as a child and released a python-covered skateboard. It immediately put her on the map. It was interesting, different, and naturally sharable; people wanted to talk about it, ride it, take pictures with it. It caused so much buzz that the *New York Times* featured it in their Sunday Style section.

The launch of Gelareh's namesake brand happened just as Instagram started to develop into a dominant social platform. As a visual person she took to the platform immediately and studied it like a lawyer preparing for the bar—except that she loved it so much it was like studying her favorite television show. She spent hour upon hour taking her highly sharable product and creating interesting, beautiful, and engaging stories to share on her feed. She also told her story and got her audience invested in her success. She lent the bags to influencers—friends of friends of friends before there was really such thing as "influencer marketing"—and it worked. She gave her creativity and time generously to her community, and they gave back their support. The online publication Fashionista celebrated these marketing efforts in an article whose banner text read: *"How handbag designer Gelareh Mizrahi used social media to increase sales by 80 percent. The young brand is a success story for using non-traditional marketing strategies—namely Instagram and strategic placement on street-style stars."* Gelareh was figuring out the new paradigm, and I had a front-row seat.

In the meantime I was the chief marketing officer of a hotel company known for innovation and creativity. Yet when I pitched non-traditional marketing methods to the management team, the response was puzzlement and disinterest. Influencers? *What are they?* Social media? *Isn't that for kids?* Content? *What are we, a movie company?* They were happy to spend hundreds of thousands of dollars on traditional marketing, succeeding only in losing market share and degrading our brand value, while at the same time Gelareh, with virtually no money, was building a brand from the ground up.

As Gelareh's business continued to grow, one holiday season we sat together and wrote out our goals. Gelareh decided she wanted a mentor—someone to help take her business to the next level—and she wanted her bags to be sold in one of the biggest and best stores in New York, a marquee account. She wrote out the name of the store, hoped, and prayed. A few months later, through Instagram and the recommendation of a friend, she met Stacy Caldwell. Stacy had just come off a stint at a major fashion house and was looking to invest her time in helping some small brands grow. Stacy agreed to work with Gelareh under an arrangement that her small business and our small family could afford. A couple of months later Stacy was able to land a meeting with Barneys New York, the holy grail for a young designer. A seal of approval from Barneys would mean the brand had officially arrived—and, yes, Barneys was the name of the store Gelareh had written down.

At the time Gelareh was pregnant with our second child, Teddy. I remember we were driving in Soho when Gelareh got the email. *Barneys had placed an order!* All their stores in the United States and in Japan would eventually carry Gelareh Mizrahi handbags. We cried. We screamed. We played loud music. It was surreal. She had done it.

Gelareh's journey is an eye-opening case study as to what is possible for anyone in the Age of Ideas. Yes, she is talented, but the route she took to share this talent is open to you and me. She has a skill, a superpower, and she has been able to amplify it and manifest her power by using tools available to us all. She built her website on Wix and then Shopify. She uses Instagram to market her business. She found her producer on Alibaba. She found her advisor on social media and through friends. Though things are going well—Gelareh recently opened a shop in Miami's Design District, and *Vogue* featured one of her bags as an "it" handbag in 2017—we are not moguls. Gelareh is just a hardworking person who wanted to create and share her art. Thanks to the time in which she was born, she had that opportunity and seized the moment.

There is nothing stopping any one of you from using the same model, tools, and platforms to build an enterprise based on your creative ideas and generating significant value and fulfillment in return. Now that we've talked about the Creator's Formula and the process around finding your purpose and aligning all the elements in your life around it, we'll get into some of the more practical information that will help you manifest that purpose in amazing ways.

Manifesting Magic in The Age of Ideas

The real magic is in making the intangible idea, the creative impulse, manifest and live in our reality.

—Mark Ryan, actor

In the past, the journey of manifesting could have taken decades or even a lifetime, but in the Age of Ideas the timeline to go from idea to product has been reduced to months, weeks, or sometimes even days. Three principle elements of the manifesting process have radically altered the landscape of what is possible:

1. How you access resources and information

2. How you manifest your ideas

3. How you share your ideas via marketing and advertising

As is obvious, how we access information and resources has been completely turned on its head. Before the web, research was time-consuming and often expensive. Just as often it was limited in scope and had a local quality, and most transactions involved middlemen. If you needed to hire a graphic designer, for instance, you had to go to a reputable agency that offered those services. Not only did that agency charge you a premium for access to their talent, but they were the gatekeepers, so they figured out ways to charge you for a lot of other things, from account reps to expensive lunches to their office rent. That made the accepted cost of business significantly higher. But in the Age of Ideas, everyone has equal access and a direct line to the talent or service you may require, which is much cheaper. And on the flip side, of course, if your business is a service business, you can present yourself to customers by using a web-building platform like Squarespace, Wix, or Wordpress to set up a storefront within a few days, without even knowing how to program.

Manifesting your ideas is also much easier. In the industrial age, you needed to own the means of production or be able to place very large and expensive orders to be able to manufacture a product; today, the means of production are much more accessible and affordable. The cost of manufacturing has dropped dramatically since the days of Henry Ford—at first due to the industrial growth of countries like China and India, and more recently because, again, the middlemen can be cut out. Even after places like China became options, you still had to fly there, strike a deal, and have significant start-up capital, but today you can just go on a platform like Alibaba or Etsy and find hundreds of factories, designers, and craftspeople willing to bid for your business and manufacture your dream. If you wanted to be in the T-shirt, shoe, or pool floatie business, you could more than likely be ready to start selling on your website in less than a month.

And finally, sharing—a/k/a marketing, advertising, and communicating—has evolved in the same way. Whether you're using Instagram, email newsletters, Google Adwords, or YouTube, the communication platforms are for the most part free to use, with the majority offering both organic (i.e. free) and paid options. Your energy can go to creating an offering that is naturally sharable and generates interesting content that can be used to cultivate your audience. Set your sights on telling a good story through photos, videos, articles, advertisements, and other creative forms of communication to incite an action from your audience.

This kind of content is necessary given the sprawl and behavior of the Internet. It's like a massive mousetrap. Users wander about consuming information, and millions of entities vie for attention through different forms of marketing. Sure, users can turn off things they don't want to see, but marketers have many more tools to refine their messages and create subtle presence. Their goal is to lead consumers down a "purchase funnel" from awareness (you know they exist), to intention (you plan to take an action), to sale (you buy something or take their desired engagement action). All of which makes the Internet just a game intent on selling users anything they could ever want or need. So the best way to stand out in this colossal marketplace is to make impactful creative content and combine it with a disciplined commitment to data analytics, magic, and math. Tell an engaging story, see how people react to it in real time, and adjust the story to achieve your desired outcome.

SIMPLE PURCHASE FUNNEL

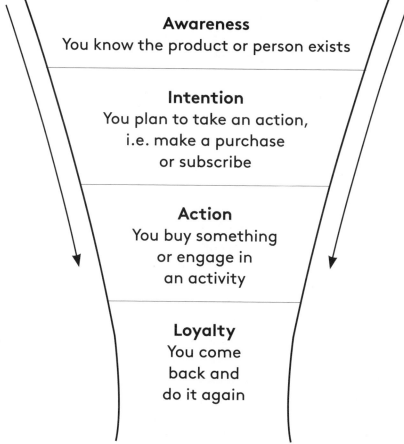

Awareness
You know the product or person exists

Intention
You plan to take an action,
i.e. make a purchase
or subscribe

Action
You buy something
or engage in
an activity

Loyalty
You come
back and
do it again

Will it be easy? No. Will it take time? Yes, probably more than you think. You will have to persevere through ups and downs, surmount unexpected obstacles, and overcome many mistakes. But if you choose the right challenge, focus your energy on your superpowers, execute at a high level, and choose the right partners and platforms, you can achieve a level of fulfillment far beyond your expectations.

THE PRINCIPLES OF MANIFESTING

Believe

Manifesting starts with believing. Pablo Picasso's mother said to him, "If you are a soldier, you will become a general. If you are a monk, you will become the Pope." Instead, he became a painter, and eventually became "Picasso." But he wasn't anointed Picasso when he woke up one morning. He became Picasso after years of art school, brushes with severe poverty, decades of hard work, and a bunch of luck. He became Picasso because he believed he could become Picasso, despite those obstacles. He manifested his creativity because despite every challenge he encountered, he continued to believe in himself and his vision. This same principle applies to your journey.

You must believe.

Ninety-nine percent of the stories we tell ourselves are limiting. While they satisfy our sense of self-importance by explaining our past, they set limits on what we believe is possible for our future. These narratives define how we think about ourselves, which directly impacts what we're capable of manifesting. But there's good news: these stories are completely made up. You can change the story any time you like.

It's generally accepted that action is what makes successful people different. What not everyone considers is that action is preceded by thought, and how successful people think is what truly differentiates them from everyone else. Successful people *believe*. They believe in themselves, they believe in their people, and, most importantly, they believe that no matter what happens, they'll figure things out. As Steve Jobs said, "When you grow up you tend to get told the world is the way it is and your life is just to live your life inside the world. Try not to bash into the walls too much. Try to have a nice family life, have fun, save a little money. That's a very limited life. Life can be much broader once you discover one simple fact: Everything around you that you call life was made up by people that were no smarter than you."

Stay Within Your Flow

It was the summer of 1947 when Harry Snyder, a World War II veteran, wandered into a Seattle restaurant and fell in love with his waitress, Esther. She'd recently graduated college with a degree in zoology but also had a strong affinity for the culinary arts. On Esther's break, they sat together in a diner booth, shared a hamburger, and discovered they both wanted to move to California. Ten months later, married, they pooled their resources, relocated to L.A., and opened a little burger joint across the street from Harry's childhood home. The fast-food business was taking off at the time—McDonald's had arrived locally just a few years earlier—but the Snyders' establishment stood out: utilizing a two-way intercom, it was the first "drive-thru" burger experience in California, aptly named In-N-Out.

Fast-forward seventy years. In-N-Out has grown to 300-plus locations and employs more than 18,000 people. While that's significant growth, it's paltry compared to the 36,000 McDonald's locations and 420,000 employees, or Starbucks' 240,000 locations and 280,000 employees. The reason behind this measured growth is that In-N-Out has consciously resisted franchising its operations or going public.

All In-N-Out restaurants are west of the Mississippi River, no more than a day's drive from their regional distribution centers. This makes it possible for the company to control the quality of their product by serving only fresh, unfrozen burgers and buns. It also allows them to control the quality of the experience, with rigorous training and people standards. Furthermore, the selective nature of their locations has led people to put an even greater emotional value on their delicious burgers. For years, customers have been begging In-N-Out to expand beyond its comfort zone, to cash in and follow society's belief that bigger is always better. But instead, the company's founding family has exhibited uncompromising discipline, remaining true to their core values and focusing on quality over quantity. This commitment to staying within their flow—concentrating their energy on a singular pursuit—has created a business that feeds itself through fierce customer loyalty and word-of-mouth marketing. In-N-Out is a great product that sells itself.

We all receive a daily barrage of messages trying to influence our actions and distract us from what's most important to us. But if we hope to manifest our creative potential, it's critical that we tune out these messages and stay within our flow. Anything that distracts us from getting closer to our true purpose diminishes the likelihood that we'll reach the pinnacle of achievement we seek. Or to quote Harry Snyder: "Keep it real simple. Do one thing and do it the best you can."

Empathy Precedes

Three centuries ago, the Baal Shem Tov, a rabbi and mystic, was in need of some assistance. A widow in his village was destitute, living in a one-room home with three children, unable to afford heat or food for her family. Desperate to get the woman some help, he went to see a wealthy friend. When he arrived at the man's doorstep, he knocked politely and said he needed to speak with him. Immediately, the friend invited the Baal Shem Tov to come in. He politely declined. "No, please, while it is so kind of you to invite me in, I must speak with you outside." The man was surprised, but held the Baal Shem Tov in high regard, so he immediately joined him outside in the cold and snow. After a few minutes of small talk, the man was shivering, barely able to feel his hands. Only then did the Baal Shem Tov ask him to help the woman and her family. The man listened intently to the request and quickly agreed to assist. The Baal Shem Tov thanked his friend for his generosity, and the man quickly ran inside to the warmth of his home. Before the Baal Shem Tov departed, though, the man reopened the door and said, "Can I ask you one question? Why did you make me come outside?" The Baal Shem Tov replied, "Empathy."

Empathy—our ability to understand and feel the experience of another—is often overlooked as a soft skill, a touchy-feely emotional construct that exists in the world of human resources, philosophy, or psychology, not the boardroom. But empathy is actually one of the most vital skills you can acquire. Your ability to empathize could very well be the difference between your success and failure.

Let me explain.

Think of yourself as Amazon during the dawn of e-commerce. You're trying to determine how and why people will shop online as opposed to at brick-and-mortar retailers, but you haven't yet figured it out. You have resources and you're great executors, but neither matter unless you create the right product and solve the right problem.

As you move forward and try to predict the future of commerce, what's the most important exercise for you to perform? How can you determine what the customer wants before they know themselves?

Empathize.

The Amazon team took on the perspective of the consumer; they felt what the consumer was feeling. By experiencing the problem from the vantage of the people dealing with it, they invented the most effective solution. For example, one-click purchases are the result of the company's obsession with a frictionless user experience. Why did they become obsessed? They experienced friction when trying to make purchases and empathized, realizing if they could make the friction for online purchases less than the friction for brick-and-mortar purchases, they would gain a sustainable competitive advantage. So that's exactly what they did.

When you find your one thing to do well, empathy is one of your most important tools. Empathy makes you understand. And understanding reveals your path.

The story behind Spanx is no different. Founder Sara Blakely didn't just have an epiphany one day and start making incredibly successful undergarments. Her empathy gave her a unique perspective and advantage, preceding her invention. Sara was selling fax machines door-to-door and was forced to wear panty hose in the hot Florida weather. While she disliked wearing them, she liked the way their control top made her body appear firmer. She realized the hosiery industry was overseen solely by men, who weren't users of the products and therefore had limited empathy for the female consumer. On the contrary, Sara had substantial empathy. This led her to understand their needs more deeply, giving her a significant advantage when she decided to design her own product.

To effectively serve the needs of another, you must understand their needs. The deeper you're able to understand and connect, the more empathy you have for their problem, the more profound your impact will be.

The Experts Are Wrong

Innovation is the act of applying your creativity to discover new and often better methods of solving problems. The innovator manifests an idea into a good or service to create greater value.

Innovators create new things. They manifest what hadn't previously existed.

Experts are individuals or groups who have comprehensive and authoritative knowledge in a particular subject. Experts have acquired their knowledge through study and practice, usually over a long period of time.

Experts reinforce the past, the tried and true.

It's generally accepted that the opinions of experts are valuable and correct. After all, they've spent lots of time studying and experiencing history.

The problem is, the future always looks different from the past.

Venture capitalist Naval Ravikant explains this phenomenon quite well:

"Before Netscape came along back in the mid-nineties it was believed that there wasn't much money to be made in Internet or Internet-type products. Before Microsoft came along it was believed that the money was in hardware not in software. Before Apple and a few other computer companies came along, it was believed that the money was in mainframes and enterprise, not in consumer. Before Uber came along it was believed that the money was in all-virtual and software and not in handling real-world things like taxi dispatchers and dealing with unions and those types of things. The conventional wisdom is always wrong."

The practice of innovating—creating new things—is future-focused. To innovate, create, or disrupt, you must, by definition, do something different. This inherently requires that you contradict the consensus opinion. And since all projects, practices, and processes are constantly evolving, all the assessments by experts—the people forming the consensus view—will eventually be outdated.

Evolution Not Revolution

Now we're going to add a twist to this idea of innovation. And we're going to do so by revisiting our trusty friend the hamburger. If you take some time to count all the burger restaurants, it will blow your mind. Along with In-N-Out and McDonald's, Burger King has over 15,000 locations. Wendy's has over 5,000. And even with the 56,000-plus restaurants between these four brands, there was enough demand in the market for Shake Shack. They've opened 136 locations since 2004.

And it doesn't stop there.

There is BurgerFi, Burger Joint, Smashburger, J. G. Melon, Five Guys, Fatburger, Johnny Rockets, P. J. Clarke's, Umami Burger, White Castle, Bill's, and many, many, many more. And it's not as if you can't get a good burger in most restaurants serving standard American fare.

How does this make sense?

Don't people crave something different, something new?

Isn't variety the spice of life?

It turns out that isn't entirely true. An overwhelming majority of successful businesses in general, and restaurants specifically, serve and sell items that are familiar. For the most part, in fact, the point of innovation or differentiation lies in the creative execution of a familiar form, not in the creation of an entirely new form.

For instance, the Cronut. Dominique Ansel didn't create something new; he combined two familiar forms in a new way. He did the same thing with milk and cookies, transforming the familiar chocolate chip cookie into a cup and then filling it with flavored milk. Ansel successfully expressed his personal creative vision through a familiar form.

The same could be said of boutique hotels, Airbnb, Uber, Instagram, and many of the most innovative companies in the world. They are all branded reinterpretations or use-changes applied to familiar forms. We rarely experience complete disruptions, such as the communication revolution brought about by social media, or the industrial revolution ushered in by the factory system and later the assembly line.

Humans are more comfortable with evolution than revolution. We crave the familiar. We want to be comfortable, we want to understand, we embrace nostalgia, and we're always trying to find our way back to our home, to the familiar.

While I believe deeply that to achieve your success, you must create something that's unique, different, and special, something that reflects your true self, for it to resonate with your audience and gain traction, the form and presentation must be familiar.

Innovation = Familiar Form + Improved Usage Model

Practical Magic

Keeping our bedrock principles of manifesting in mind, now let's get into some practical information, starting with a step-by-step look at how to manifest your ideas.

Step #1: Define Your Concept

The first step when manifesting an idea is to marry the emotional and practical elements of your idea into a defined concept. If you've worked through the process in Parts 2 and 3, you know your purpose and have a clear, concise statement of that purpose—one that should be entirely emotional. Now you need to connect that emotional purpose with a practical application.

As an example, let's look back at Ikea. Their purpose is to "*create a better everyday life*" for many, but their concept is to "*support this vision by offering a wide range of well-designed, functional home furnishing products at prices so low that as many people as possible will be able to afford them.*" While the two are related, they are quite different. One is a **feeling**, and the other is an **offering**.

Purpose Statement = Emotional
Concept Description = Practical

INNOVATION

=

Familiar Form

+

Improved Usage Model

4 STEPS TO MANIFESTING YOUR IDEA

1 Define Your Concept

2 Create Your Brand

3 Build Your Product & Storefront

4 Embrace Uncertainty & Fear

To define your concept, write down two to three simple, clear sentences describing what you are trying to create. The best way to do that is to write down everything in your mind without overthinking or letting the monkey-mind limit or confuse you. You know your purpose; just let the concept that comes from that purpose flow.

Write Concept Description Below

_____

_____

_____

_____

_____

Once you have done this, refine your concept description by considering the following questions:

1. Is this aligned with my purpose statement?
2. If not, how can I align it with my purpose?
3. Is this my highest and best challenge right now?
4. How can I set this up in a way where I can meet my short-term and long-term needs while making it a reality?

Let's look at an example. Say you wanted to open a fried-chicken restaurant. Well, the first question would be: What makes your fried-chicken shop different from other such shops? We call this your unique value proposition, or UVP. For our purposes, let's use the following features as the ones creating your chicken shop's UVP:

1. We only serve chicken fingers.

2. We have 20 homemade sauces.

3. We use organic farm-raised chickens.

4. We only do takeout and delivery, no in-store dining.

5. We employ former foster children for all non-managerial positions.

With this in mind, your concept description would be as follows:

We are opening a casual, quick-service chicken restaurant specializing in organic chicken fingers served with our one-of-a-kind homemade sauces. The restaurant will focus on take-out/pick-up and delivery business. Our service staff will be made up of former foster children, 18-24 years of age, in order to provide them the necessary skills to succeed both personally and professionally and give back to the community.

Most people never even get to the point of defining their concept. They get so excited about an idea that they start the process of creating without ever truly defining their UVP—without seeing if it aligns with their purpose and understanding if demand exists in the market. But your road to successfully manifesting your idea starts at the seed level: thought must precede action, and understanding what makes you different from everyone and everything else in *your* world is critical to creating something truly special.

Note: By referring to YOUR world instead of THE world, we are making a critical distinction. You don't need to be the best in the world at what you do—you need to be the best in the world in which you are doing business. For example, let's say you opened a North Carolina brewery; you don't need to be the best brewery in America or the world to succeed, but only in your competitive zone, such as the state of North Carolina, or the Southeast United States. Then you set up the business plan to maximize your likelihood of success in that specific region. Defining your competitive zone is crucial, and when you are the best in YOUR world, the likelihood of greatness in THE world goes up exponentially.

Concept Exercise:

Have an idea? Take a moment to refine your concept description now. Make sure to ask all the right questions and share your description with some people you trust.

_____

_____

_____

_____

_____

_____

_____

Step #2: Creating Your Brand

The degree of trust I feel towards a product, rather than an assessment of its features and benefits, will determine whether I'll buy this product or that.

—Marty Neumeier, author and branding expert

The next step in the manifesting process is to create your brand. What that means is taking your practical concept statement and turning it into a combination of:

VISUALS
The way it looks

VALUES
The way it feels and acts

VOCALS
The way it speaks

More specifically, that means items like a logo, tagline, core values, and any other creative outputs (such as videos) that capture the essence of the message, feelings, and user experience you are trying to create. These visuals, values, and words together will create a brand that you will eventually turn into an actual product.

An easy way to understand visuals, values, and vocals is to compare yourself with friends or family. What makes you different? How you dress, your outfits, your hair, your glasses, how you sign your name—these are your visuals. What is important to you that may not be important to everyone else? These are your values. And how you speak, these are your vocals. Together these make up who you are. For a company, it's their brand. For instance:

Richard Branson and Virgin are rebellious change-makers.

Timberland and Patagonia are adventurous explorers.

Mercedes and Ritz-Carlton are stable, old-guard rulers.

Campbell's is a comforting caregiver.

Nike is the hero, the victor.

These brands didn't always represent these archetypes—they didn't always make people *feel*. They acquired that power over time by consistently delivering on their point of difference, their UVP. That consistent difference resulted in a distinct feeling among their audience. And that feeling will eventually be the emotional part of your brand, which exists right now only in your mind. When enough people feel one way about you, they become your community or tribe. The tribe validates the brand. Or as Amazon founder Jeff Bezos put it, "A brand for a company is like a reputation for a person. You earn reputation by trying to do hard things well."

Few companies execute that better than Starbucks. Originally, they were just a place to get coffee, a basic commodity. But over time, and consistently, Starbucks made people *feel* their point of difference. Eventually, we all knew what to expect from them, and they gained our trust. Now, we can get an Iced Green Tea anywhere in the world and feel that combination of familiarity, aspiration, and caffeine that so many of us crave. And we're willing to pay a premium for the trust that comes with that consistency.

Brand Exercise #1:

To determine your brand, as an individual or an organization, try answering the following questions:

Who are you?

Example: We're Starbucks, a multinational coffeehouse experience.

What do you do?

We're not just passionate purveyors of coffee, we supply everything else that goes with a full and rewarding coffee-house experience. We also offer a selection of premium teas, fine pastries, and other delectable treats to please the taste buds.

Why does it matter? (VALUES)

Every day, we go to work hoping to do two things: share great coffee with our friends and help make the world a little better. A place for conversation and a sense of community. We inspire and nurture the human spirit—one person, one cup, and one neighborhood at a time.

What does it look like? (VISUALS)

Brand Exercise #2:

To express and share your brand I recommend you make a CON-CEPT DECK. We're talking about a simple document, 1-2 written pages, or, as a presentation, 8-10 slides (the type is bigger, don't be intimidated), that you can share with others and consistently refine to describe your idea.

In a Word, PowerPoint, or Keynote document fill in the following outline, either as bullet points or slides:

1. **Title:** *Brand Name/Logo*

2. **Purpose Statement:** *Create a better everyday life for many.*

3. **Concept Description:** *We are opening a quick-service chicken restaurant specializing in organic chicken fingers served with our one-of-a-kind homemade sauces. The restaurant will focus on take-out/pick-up and delivery business. Our staff will be made up of former foster children, 18-24 years of age, in order to give back to the community and provide them the necessary skills to succeed both personally and professionally.*

4. **Unique Value Proposition:** *List out the key differentiating points about what you are trying to create:*

   a. *We only serve chicken fingers.*

   b. *We have 20 homemade sauces.*

   c. *We only use organic farm-raised chickens.*

   d. *We only do takeout and delivery.*

   e. *We employ former foster children.*

5. **Core Values:** *List the key attributes you would like people to feel about your business. For example, "always fresh and friendly."*

6. **Visuals:** *Go on Instagram, Pinterest, Google images, Behance, or other platforms and find pictures, logos, and sayings that you believe capture the essence of what you are trying to create. Save these images on your computer and select the best ones. Add those to your deck to provide an idea of the "look and feel" of your brand.*

7. **Target Audience:** *The demographic or psychographic you are trying to reach. For example, young adults interested in street style and entrepreneurship between the ages of 25-40 years old. Or, people who believe that the*

government should be smaller and we should pay less in taxes, a/k/a Republicans (a psychographic).

Once this document is complete, engage a graphic designer. They can be found through a friend, on Behance, Fiverr, Craigslist, or at a local university or coworking space. Ask the designer to help you refine your presentation into a simple, visually compelling explanation of your product or service. We will refer to this as your concept deck. Ideally the designer will also help you with the creation of a logo mark. While this may cost a few extra dollars, it will be valuable when interacting with potential customers, partners, or investors. Remember, perception is reality.

Congrats! You are on your way.

Step #3: Build Your Product & Storefront

The ultimate step in your manifesting process is to take your brand and turn it into a product and your storefront(s).

Your product is a good, idea, method, information, or service created as a result of a process that serves a need or satisfies a want. It has a combination of tangible and intangible attributes (benefits, features, functions, uses) that a seller offers a buyer for purchase.

Your storefront is your website, app, or presence on a platform such as eBay, Amazon, etsy, or iTunes, where you can sell your goods, services, or content.

Now is when you take your defined idea and start turning it into something real and sharable. For instance, if you want to start a T-shirt company, this is the stage where you have your T-shirts designed, find a manufacturer, and put them up for sale on your storefront, i.e. your website. We will get into *how* to share in the next section, Strategic Sharing, but before you share your idea you have to make it real.

Will your product be perfect at first? No. Will it fly off your website on day one? Probably not. The manifesting process is iterative. In the Age of Ideas you bring something to market, test it, analyze the response, and continuously refine. It is an ongoing feedback loop—share, listen, refine. The difference is that today the feedback loop is much shorter and more accurate: the everyday entrepreneur has access to data analytics platforms they can use on their websites to help them identify opportunities and mistakes and make changes to their products and platform almost instantly. It used to be that if you designed the store wrong you were screwed, but today you can test five homepages on your website and optimize performance in real time. Make some T-shirts, send an email or share them with people you trust, and get their reactions. Or build a website and have people try it out, see what journey they take and analyze where they drop off. The more interactions you have, the closer you will get to something that works—we call "something that works" a product-market fit.

The key to successfully manifesting is perseverance. Most people quit when the feedback is not good or things get difficult. Those who succeed are the ones who can overcome pain; they get past it by realizing it is not a statement about their self-worth. They continue to believe in themselves and their ideas and trust that, whatever mistakes they make, they will figure it out.

The Product

While some businesses may require physical locations, such as retail shops, offices, or factories, the majority of businesses today are housed virtually. Whether you are manufacturing a product or providing a service, in the modern market products should be tested in the virtual marketplace prior to existing in the experiential marketplace. For example, if you wanted to make a new hot sauce, you could produce a small quantity and offer it for sale to both retailers and wholesalers on your website. After you gauge the market demand, you can then decide the best secondary methods of distribution. This was not possible prior to the Age of Ideas.

The same strategy can apply to professional service providers and freelancers, from artists to writers to accountants. Why do you need a physical office when you can put your service online, generate leads, and start by taking meetings at a coworking space or even a coffee shop? Even if your product is an experiential or retail-based business, you can still test it with a pop-up or mobile shop prior to going all in on a retail location. Ali Webb and her partners started Dry Bar, a hair salon focusing on blow-drying hair, with a mobile blow-dry truck. The demand for the service was off the charts, so

FEEDBACK LOOP

Share

Present your product, service, or content to the market

Listen

Observe reactions both anecdotally and through analytic platforms

Refine

Adjust the necessary aspects to achieve product-market fit after a lot of strategic consideration they opened their first retail location. Now they have over seventy Dry Bar locations.

The Storefront

With this in mind, building your storefont is the next step in the manifesting process. A storefront, again, refers to your website, app, or presence on an existing service such as eBay or Amazon. A website is the ideal environment to refine your brand and product, from user experience to visuals to pricing. You will be able to test everything in real time, sharing with those you trust and actively interacting with the marketplace. Your mantra should be *refine, refine, refine*, until you find the best expression of yourself and your idea, the product-market fit.

Since you will have completed your concept deck, it will be very easy for you to create your website, as the website is just a more developed expression of that deck. It's the same information, adjusted for a different audience. Your concept deck is for collaborators and investors (B2B), while your website is for customers (B2C). The most cost-effective method is a do-it-yourself service like Squarespace, Wix, or Wordpress. Personally I like to spend a bit more money to work with a low-cost programmer, but these DIY services provide easy-to-use templates that allow you to design your own professional-looking website and have it up and running quickly. They also offer simplified tools for things like search engine optimization (SEO) and analytics that are fairly easy to engage with even as a beginner.

If you want to have e-commerce on your storefront, these services can also be user-friendly, but there are more robust services that specialize in e-commerce, like Shopify. If you are willing to invest a bit more money—at least $1,000—you can find a web designer who can build a simple and beautiful website for you. Be aware that when using a designer, you should assume there will also be some ongoing maintenance costs. With that said, website costs are continuing to drop, and today, even fairly complex website tech can be addressed by the plethora of "off the shelf" plug-ins that exist for most functions. There is little difference between independent web developers and high-cost agencies charging tens of thousands of dollars. While Target or JetBlue may require dozens of people to manage their web business, you probably do not. You should be focused on building your MVP—minimum viable product—for the lowest possible cost, and then you can evaluate the response of your audience or trusted advisors before you invest further.

Note: Your goal is a **creative monopoly**, which we define as an innovative or creative individual or company with a sustainable competitive edge. Because a monopoly has no competition, it can maximize profits by controlling supply and price. There is only one you, so when you amplify your purpose to its purest form, you will have exclusive control of a product or service in a particular market. The artist Jeff Koons has a creative monopoly; no one else can create a Koons piece, and his team controls the supply of his work coming to market. Google is also an example of a creative monopoly—it controls 80 percent of the search market, which allows it to control the supply and cost of advertising inventory. And it relies on technology it created for its monopoly. Be aware that if your edge is technology-based, heavy investment will probably be required to maintain your monopoly, contrary to the examples mentioned in the previous paragraphs.

Once you have a product and a storefront, you are in business—as an entrepreneur, as a writer, as whatever you say you are, because that is how the modern paradigm works. It doesn't mean you are *good* at what you say you do; few people are when they are just starting something, even something that reflects their true purpose and passion. But you are in the game, on the road to becoming better (if you integrate your life, understand your biases, and have chosen the right challenge), and if you keep at it, you can become great, maybe even the best in your world. But remember, be honest and be true to your purpose. The market will know if you are not, and your products will not resonate with your audience. Most importantly, you won't be fulfilled. It always comes back to this:

Your Defined Purpose

+

Your Unique Talent

=

A Sustainable
Competitive Advantage
& Lasting Fulfillment

The more energy you put in, the more energy you will get out. Or as the Beatles put it, the love you take is equal to the love you make.

Step #4: Embracing Uncertainty & Fear

My life has been a path at the edge of uncertainty. Today, I think we educate kids to be settled in the comfortable chair. You have your job, you have your little car, you have a place to sleep and the dreams are dead. You grow on a secure path. All of us should conquer something in life and it needs a lot of work and it needs a lot of risk. In order to grow and to improve you have to be there at the edge of uncertainty.

—Francis Mallmann, chef, restaurateur, author

Uncertainty has negative connotations. It's defined as a situation with unknown or imperfect information. Being uncertain of your goals or direction is frowned upon in our society.

Possibility has positive connotations. It's defined as something that's able to be done or within your power or capacity to do. Possibilities are exciting.

Uncertainty is the glass half empty. Possibility is the glass half full.

They mean the same thing, just from different perspectives. But whatever your perspective, avoiding uncertainty limits what's possible, while embracing uncertainty makes everything possible.

Embracing uncertainty is precisely what enables some individuals and organizations to realize their potential. The idea is to exist within a distinct balance: you must be absolutely certain in your overarching purpose and confident in your abilities, while also knowing you will have to deal with the unexpected. You have to shut down the fear that comes from that knowledge, as it can lead to making short-term decisions that limit long-term prospects. Know in your heart that you will succeed, but accept that your path will be unclear and at times invisible.

While this way of thinking is illogical, it's important to note that by definition, unbelievable achievement is illogical. It isn't logical to think you'll create a multibillion-dollar company where nothing previously existed. It isn't logical to think that one day your paintings will hang in a museum and be priceless. It isn't logical to think that millions of people will buy your records and come to see you perform. Yet these things happen, and it's when things are the most uncertain that the most possibility exists. Think of it like risk and reward. As RZA of the Wu-Tang Clan explains, "Confusion is a gift from God. Those times when you feel most desperate for a solution, sit. Wait. The information will become clear. The confusion is there to guide you." I cannot tell you how many times I have reminded myself of this concept and benefited from not taking action until I reached a deeper level of clarity.

Uncertainty and fear are first cousins. They go hand in hand, trying to distract you from your ultimate goals. But manifesting is the fun part—it's the point in your process when you finally get into your flow and begin to see your dreams come to life. It's also the part of our process when you're exposing the most intimate parts of yourself. Whenever that happens, a natural fear occurs, and in order to manifest effectively and to your greatest potential, you must embrace that fear instead of running from it. You can't allow it to stop you from sharing what means the most to you.

While this may be easier said than done, the most effective method I know for embracing fear is understanding its nature. Fear is our most instinctive method of protection. On the most basic, animal level, when you find yourself in the kind of situation where you've been hurt in the past, you are fearful. While that may some-times be irrational, just think what would happen if that instinct didn't exist: you would burn your hand on a hot pot and then go back and burn your hand again the next time. Yet this stroke of evolutionary genius is also a major roadblock in our path to higher consciousness and achievement. In order to attain a level of con-sciousness where we can manifest unbelievable success, we must confront and overcome our fear.

Let's explore fear further through the lens of "emotional labor." For most of us, the journey to manifesting our potential will be a journey of *emotional* labor, engaging with and managing our emotions throughout a long process of creation, rejection, and improvement. A perfect metaphor for this emotional labor is the experience of overcoming a challenge through physical labor, such as learning to shoot a basketball. When you first try to shoot a basketball, inevitably you will experience the challenge of missing many more shots than you make. But Steph Curry didn't become the greatest shooter of all time by quitting when he missed; instead he shot the ball thousands of more times until he reached his goal, paying close attention to WHY he failed and moving through it and refining his process. That is how you become great, by confronting your fears every day and overcoming the pain or embarrassment or frustration until you reach your goal. As Curry's college coach pointed out, the future Golden State star was consistently the "hardest-working player" with a "fire that raged within him." Steph Curry confronted his fears every day.

We must apply the same dedicated approach to our emotional labor. As you manifest your purpose every day, you will experience fear—fear of rejection, fear of failure, fear of standing out. As Seth Godin puts it, "The difficult task [with emotional labor] is confronting the fear of failure. That is what we are paid to do, that is what we are rewarded for." That's it. Throughout the process you must accept your fear and not let it distract you from what you must do to achieve true and lasting fulfillment. Or as our friend Seth puts it, you must "dance with the fear."

Free To Fail

Ted Williams was an exceptional baseball player. During his nineteen years playing for the Boston Red Sox, he made seventeen trips to the All-Star Game, was twice named the American League MVP, was the batting champion six times, and won the Triple Crown twice. At the end of his career, he had a .344 batting average, with 521 home runs. Most legendarily of all, in 1941, Williams ended his season with a .406 average, making him the last player ever to hit over .400 for a season. Ted Williams is without a doubt "the greatest hitter who ever lived."

Now let's take a look at Williams's statistics from a different perspective. Although he was baseball's all-time greatest hitter, he was only successful at getting a hit 34.5 percent of the time. That means the best-ever batter failed more than 65 percent of the time throughout his career. For every attempt he made, two out of three times, he failed.

But maybe that's just baseball. Let's check the application of this theory in another sport. The greatest basketball player of all time is Michael Jordan. MJ had a career field-goal percentage of 49.7 percent. This means that half of the time, when the greatest player and most prolific scorer in basketball history took a shot, he missed. One out of every two attempts, he failed.

Okay, but what about the world beyond sports?

Michael Jackson recorded and released approximately 225 songs. Jackson is recognized as one of the most prolific hit-makers in pop-music history, yet of his 200-plus recorded songs, only two out of every ten cracked the top 40 (with thirteen going to number one).

Now, let's look at these statistics in a different context: your work. If you told your boss or coworkers you were going to fail 50 percent of the time like Michael Jordan, 65 percent of the time like Ted Williams, or 80 percent of the time like Michael Jackson, do you think you would be looked upon favorably? The answer is without a doubt no. We're taught to believe that mistakes are bad, and that when you fail, you're considered a failure. This simply isn't true. Without failure and mistakes, it's impossible to become great and achieve something different, special, or innovative. It's like cooking; the first time you make something, you might fail—it might not come together—but with experimentation and practice, it often becomes great. I'm not advocating that you bet your future or your organization's future on moonshot ideas. What I am expressing is the belief that we must encourage, not punish, experimentation, exploration, and learning through experience.

Pixar is the closest thing in modern business to Ted Williams, Michael Jordan, or Michael Jackson. At the time I am writing this they've released twenty movies since their inception, and every single one of them has been a commercial and critical success. Surprisingly, underlying their nearly perfect record is the fervent belief that it must be safe to make mistakes or fail. Pixar's founder Ed Catmull said, "Failure isn't a necessary evil. In fact it's not evil at all. It is a necessary consequence of doing something new." He continued by saying, "Similarly, it is not the manager's job to prevent risks. It is the manager's job to make it safe to take them."

In other words, to achieve unbelievable success, we must create an environment where experimentation and the occasional failure are permitted and encouraged. Failure is painful, and our feelings about this pain confuse our understanding of its worth. We must learn to separate the good and the bad feelings related to failure and accept it as a critical component on our journey to greatness. Embrace uncertainty; dance with your fear. Because you will fail—but it is only failure if you fail to learn from each attempt.

Don't Quit Your Dayjob

While it is essential to embrace uncertainty, I am not advocating quitting your day job. That would be foolish. As Maslow said, we can't engage in the process of becoming fully self-actualized unless our basic needs are met—food, shelter, clothing. You are NOT free to fail if failing means being unable to support yourself or your family. And manifesting magic does not mean you will start making money immediately; it most likely will take years of hard work and many failures along the way.

For most of us, that means pursuing our purpose, at least at the start, as a side hustle. That may mean waking up earlier, working later, or setting aside time on the weekend to advance your ideas and begin the process of making them manifest. This book, for instance, took me five years to write—not because I am a slow writer, but because it could not be my sole focus. I wrote parts one and two over the course of a year, and then I began writing a weekly newsletter to build an audience and test my material in front of an audience. I refined each section of the book with an editor, reorganized it, rethought it, and honed its focus for another few years. During that time my wife gave birth to two children and built her own business; we moved to another state; I started a new C-level job at a multi-billion dollar company. I promise you, I had very little time. But I carved out every moment I could, because this is my purpose—I knew I needed to share this information—and I was committed to manifesting it in the world.

Maybe one day this project will be able to provide my family enough revenue to support our daily existence, but until then I've taken enormous satisfaction in the process of pursuing my purpose. Though I've wrestled with many moments of frustration, delays, setbacks, revisions, and so on, it has provided me with emotional fulfillment far beyond my expectations.

Your process will have many of the same ups and downs. The key is to dive into it and trust that the universe wants what is best for you. Eventually.

Some Days Will Suck

Some days will suck.

Some weeks will be hard.

Some months will be filled with doubt, fear, and the terror of not knowing.

There's no way around it. I tried to avoid the pain, the struggle, and the sacrifice; it didn't work.

There are no shortcuts.

Those brave enough to face the pain and struggle are the ones who get the fulfillment. They're rewarded with the river of positive energy that can only come from overcoming a challenge.

Your fulfillment is dependent on your ability to persist. To fight through the hard times, the days you don't believe, and still have certainty you'll succeed.

You accept sacrifice when you sign up. It's in the fine print.

But don't be scared.

You know you want it. You want it all.

You want everything, so you have to be willing to give up everything.

That's why your pursuit must align with your purpose.

Your pursuit must be innately tied to your inner desires. Then, when things get really hard, when everything goes wrong, you won't quit.

You won't quit because you can't. It would be like quitting on yourself.

You will change course, you will evolve, but you won't quit.

That's what life is all about: a struggle to overcome a challenge.

Magic-makers, groundbreakers, creators, you can't avoid your calling; you can't avoid your truth.

So step forth, be brave, and take your shot.

But never forget, some days will suck.

SOME DAYS WILL SUCK
SOME DAYS WILL SUCK
SOME DAYS WILL SUCK
SOME DAYS WILL SUCK
SOME DAYS WILL SUCK
SOME DAYS WILL SUCK
SOME DAYS WILL SUCK
SOME DAYS WILL SUCK
SOME DAYS WILL SUCK
SOME DAYS WILL SUCK

THE PRINCIPLES OF SHARING

Kith

At this point I'm just doing what I like to do. People are gonna love it or hate it. But the one thing is that it's gonna be honest. And between Kith Treats and all of these nostalgic moments that we had, I'm just living a dream right now. This is what I love.

—Ronnie Fieg, founder of Kith

In the Jewish religion, a bar mitzvah is the ritual induction of a boy into manhood at the age of thirteen. It's recognized as the time when he, not his parents, becomes responsible for his actions.

Ronnie Fieg took this transition quite seriously.

Fieg's first cousin is David Z, a legendary sneaker and sportswear retailer in New York City. Ronnie's parents were paying off his bar mitzvah celebration with the gifts from the guests, and as is customary, David came to the celebration with his gift in hand: an envelope of cash. Ronnie saw this as an opportunity and said to David, "Thanks, but no thanks; I'd rather have a job working for you instead." The next day, Ronnie started as a stock boy at David Z.

In the late 1990s, David Z was located on Eighth Street in Greenwich Village, one of the most influential blocks in the country for street culture. All the big hip-hop artists spent their weekends hanging on the block. They would start on the corner with a Gray's Papaya hot dog, maybe grab a pair of Parasuco Jeans in one of the lesser-known shops, and end up in David Z's buying a pair of GORE-TEX boots.

This was where Ronnie learned the business of sneakers and streetwear. As he tells it, "When Lauryn Hill spits 'In some Gore-Tex and sweats I make treks like I'm homeless,' the week that she recorded that album, I sold her the boots. And when you see Ma$e and Diddy in the 'Been Around the World' video and they're wearing Dolomites, I sold them their boots. Anytime you'd see Wu-Tang with custom Wallabies, I used to get them custom-made for them. Jay-Z was there every weekend. 'Cruising down Eighth Street'—when he spits that on the ['Empire State of Mind'] track, that was him every Saturday, cruising down Eighth Street. I used to help him with his Timberlands every Saturday." For Ronnie, working at David Z was like going to the Harvard of street style.

Ronnie worked his way up from stock boy to sales clerk to assistant manager to manager to assistant buyer and, eventually, buyer for multiple David Z stores around the age of twenty-five. As the head buyer, Ronnie had direct exposure to the brands, and luckily for him, David Z moved volume, which gave him influence. He formed a relationship with ASICS at a Vegas trade show, and the brand performed well in the stores, so ASICS decided to give him the opportunity to design his own silhouette.

This was propitious; back in the day, his mom had bought him a pair of ASICS Gel-Lyte IIIs at Tennis Junction in Great Neck instead of the more popular Reebok Pumps he wanted. At first, Ronnie hated them, but eventually he grew to love them, wearing them until they had "holes in the soles." He wanted to replace them, but they'd been discontinued. When ASICS gave him the chance to design his own, the Gel-Lyte III was his obvious choice. He pulled them out of the archive and created three versions, of which a total of 756 pairs were manufactured. He called in some favors from a few friends, and they threw an event at David Z. The next day, they sold a few pairs, and he shared the story of the shoes with one of the buyers. The day after that, Ronnie's mother called him, exclaiming, "Your shoe is on the cover of the *Wall Street Journal!*" The guy Ronnie had told the story to was an editor at the *WSJ*, and he wrote a story about limited-run sneakers. The next day, there was a line around the block. That same day, the president of Adidas America showed up and, as Ronnie tells it, "I told him the story, and that's how we started talking about working on a shoe called the Black Tie." Ronnie had begun to build his following.

While David Z had a thriving business focused on moving quantity, Ronnie was coming up in the era of Union and Supreme. He was obsessed with what they were doing. "What I really wanted to do is build a curated lifestyle shop, and not be pigeonholed into one category or another. [I wanted to] give [a] New York vibe [to] all types of products, multi-brand, and have our own brand." So, in 2007, he started Kith, a small T-shirt and jacket line, and in 2010 he decided he was ready to launch a Kith shop. He partnered with Sam Ben-Avraham, owner of another legendary New York retail chain, Atrium. His first shop was 800 square feet, and during development he slept in the store for five straight days. "Just building the store with our bare hands," he remembers. "I borrowed money to open the shop. It really took off the minute we opened, and the money was paid back in like four months."

Since the opening of that shop, Kith has become a retail juggernaut. Currently, the brand has seven permanent locations, along with pop-up seasonal locations in places such as Aspen. They recently quadrupled the size of the original Lafayette Street store and opened the Arsham/Feig Art Gallery on the top floor with artist Daniel Arsham, a Kith collaborator. There are also multiple locations offering their Kith Treats concept, a cereal bar that focuses on combining cereal and ice cream for decadent ice cream desserts.

Why is Kith thriving when most other retail brands are dying? The answer is that it is a highly sharable product built firmly on the pillars of the Creator's Formula.

All Kith stores are designed by Snarkitecture, a firm founded by Arsham, focused on "investigating the boundaries between art and architecture." Arsham's work makes the stores more like immersive art exhibits than retail stores, and that makes Kith a place to experience, rather than just shop. The stores are highly curated from start to finish; whether it's their sneaker displays, book selections, wallpaper, or website, everything reinforces the brand's status as a culture creator. As Ronnie puts it, "We take a lot of risks, but you have to take risks in this market to be rewarded.... You need to actually provide newness and culture-shifting ideas."

While people go to Kith for the practical reason of purchasing sneakers, they also come to be a part of the movement, to say they have been there, to take photos of themselves in the store or wearing their piece of culture. Think of today's best stores as contemporary art museums, but instead of taking photos in front of an innovative canvas or sculpture, you're taking photos in front of branded installations and products. It's a similar kind of creativity, in a different medium and setting.

Next, Ronnie made collaborating core to his operation, not a side project. He collaborates with brands ranging from the commercial (Rugrats, Power Rangers, Coca-Cola, Cap'n Crunch) to high style (Colette, BAPE, Bergdorf Goodman) to footwear legends (Nike, Timberland, Adidas). Through this process, Kith is constantly exchanging intellectual capital, social capital, and customers with some of the most influential brands and people on the planet. As Ronnie explains it, "Working with brands becomes important when [it] really represents both sides in a collaborative effort."

And because Kith is launching these collaborations throughout the year, customers always have another reason to visit or follow, as there's always something new happening.

This constant activity and content is vital in a saturated media landscape. Combined with their experiential stores, this makes Kith the ultimate naturally sharable product. It's a model that makes sure all channels, offline and online, are overflowing with great content. From the stores to the product to the partners to the cereal bar, Kith is brimming with interesting stories to tell and imagery to share, both for the traditional media and social media. And that kind of content is immensely valuable in the modern age—just take a look at the #Kith hashtag and you'll see how a sharable product can transform into a movement.

Finally, Kith is tapping into two massively cultish communities: sneaker geeks and street-style junkies. These communities are constantly looking for what's next, and Kith is always there to give it to them. Kith's followers are digital natives involved in a global conversation. Ronnie's decades of street credibility give the brand authenticity, and the market knowledge he and his team possess helps Kith stay ahead of the curve—both invaluable assets when dealing with these types of communities. More than that, popular culture pulls directly from these two fringe communities to decide what's new and next, so these communities amplify Kith's brand presence and message, allowing it to have a significant impact on the larger cultural conversation.

Kith is exciting not only because the product is great, but because the *business* is great. Ronnie Fieg and his team understand how to drive commerce via culture, by building a product that naturally fits into the cultural conversation. By investing his resources into emotionally generous creative outputs, the community naturally amplifies the message, and that is the definition of strategic sharing.

Strategic Sharing

You won't understand the unabashed power of community until you are part of one.

—Unknown

We all crave the sense of belonging that comes with being part of a community, experiencing that fellowship with others that results from sharing common interests and goals. These types of connections engage the human spirit. Habitually, we're driven to organize ourselves into groups—by industry, religion, hobby, sports teams, even the television shows we watch. Therefore, to effectively share your ideas, it's critical that you recognize the importance of communities and how they've evolved.

In the industrial age, communication was primarily a one-way road. Messages went out from those in control of the distribution channels and were consumed by the watchers and listeners. There were only a few options, no DVR, and limited places to comment or criticize. The only way to amplify your message was to spend more money on advertising. The more you spent promoting your message, the more exposure your message received. Whether or not the audience liked the message was a guessing game.

In the Age of Ideas, the cost of communicating is far less, and digitally, the reaction is instant and measurable. While you can still buy distribution, the more you advertise or sell, the less engaged the communities you reach will be. Trust has replaced money as the most valuable commodity in communication; in a saturated environment, we only pay attention to messages from sources we trust. Additionally, that one-way road has become a multi-lane expressway, with messages that are circulated and re-circulated by communities with overlapping interests. And it's clear where the power of those communities is generated.

In June 2017, Nike realigned their corporate structure to focus on twelve cities. They did this because they believe cities "will represent over 80 percent of their growth through 2020," and described the strategy as "local business, on a global scale." Translation: Nike recognized that their future sales are tied more than ever to their

STRATEGIC SHARING: PUTTING THE NEEDS AND DESIRES OF THE AUDIENCE AHEAD OF YOUR OWN— WHILE MAINTAINING YOUR INTENTION TO ACHIEVE A DESIRED OUTCOME.

social relevance in key metropolises, so they decided to concentrate their resources on influencers—not just social influencers in the traditional sense, but whole sub-cultures of influential people who live in cities. More importantly, they recognize that the people influencing culture and consuming their most profitable products are no longer citizens of countries; they're global citizens residing in a select group of cities.

While the digital revolution gave us the ability to live remotely, it also created a ravenous desire for true connection. People, young and old, want to be part of something larger than themselves; they want to live a rich life filled with shared experiences; they want variety, diversity, and energy, and cities provide these things.

At the same time, wealth is more concentrated than ever. The wealthiest among us generally live in large metropolises, and like our ancestors who settled where food or water was plentiful, we too settle where our most important resource is most abundant.

We follow the money.

This concentration of connection and capital inevitably results in cities becoming epicenters of culture and influence. Think about it—imagine being a young person watching all the amazing things happening in New York, Paris, or London on Instagram. If you're not in one of these cities, the pull to get there is strong. This urbanization movement has been happening for some time, of course, but the communications revolution has amplified the pace dramatically. It's predicted that by 2050, about 64 percent of the developing world and 86 percent of the developed world will be urbanized.

Trends are flowing more rapidly and randomly than ever before because these cities are linked in real time through social media and the Internet. This has forced a rapid, unmediated evolution of culture and trends. The only way to truly build relevance and drive sales is to focus your resources on influencing the culture within cities. As Douglas Holt writes in the *Harvard Business Review*, "Social media binds together communities that once were geographically isolated, greatly increasing the pace and intensity of collaboration. Now that these once-remote communities are densely networked, their cultural influence has become direct and substantial."

Instead of sending out one-way messages—i.e. traditional advertising—we must now relate to these overlapping communities by appealing to their shared beliefs, values, and struggles. We call this strategic sharing—putting the needs and desires of the audience ahead of your own—while maintaining your intention to achieve a desired outcome. Airbnb is a perfect example. They tapped into a global community of underserved travelers looking for a more connected, localized, and experiential way to travel. It took them years to establish the level of trust needed with their target communities, but once they did, travelers organically amplified their message. When you find the communities that share your belief system, you must contribute meaningfully and consistently. For some, this may mean sharing information or creativity, while for others it may mean throwing events or giving to charity. While it requires patience and time, anything worth doing requires that you make significant investments. This type of cultivated amplification is the result of doing the right thing over a long period of time, and consistently and strategically doing right by your audience is the special sauce of modern marketing.

But you don't have to be a global brand to apply strategic sharing. As Kevin Kelly said in his popular essay "1,000 True Fans," to make a living as "a craftsperson, photographer, musician, designer, author, animator, app maker, entrepreneur, or inventor you need only thousands of true fans. A true fan is defined as a fan that will buy anything you produce. These diehard fans will drive 200 miles to see you sing; they will buy the hardback and paperback and Audible versions of your book; they will purchase your next figurine sight unseen; they will pay for the 'best-of' DVD version of your free YouTube channel; they will come to your chef's table once a month. If you have roughly a thousand true fans like this, you can make a living."

In Manhattan's Soho district, there's a restaurant named Jack's Wife Freda that applies strategic sharing beautifully. While their food is consistent and high-quality, they aren't serving high-end cuisine and haven't spent tons of money on décor or marketing. But Jack's Wife Freda is jammed, all the time—so much so that they had to open a second location. The owners, Maya and Dean Jankelowitz, are restaurant veterans who trained for many years under the legendary restaurateur Keith McNally of Balthazar fame. They're present, attentive, nice, and involved with their community.

Their goal has always been to run a great, comfortable, and successful restaurant and take care of their regulars, a/k/a their "true fans." They've done an incredible job of tapping into overlapping communities by simply doing the right thing. Over the years, their friends and customers have become influential in the communities of fashion, art, media, and hospitality. These people posted regularly about Jack's on their social media channels, and that led hordes of young professionals to flock to the restaurant. Maya and Dean did the right thing, combined it with good strategic thinking, and over time, the communities amplified their message.

Unlocking the power of strategic sharing and your community all comes back to the quality of your contribution. The more giving you are, the more likely a community will embrace your message and amplify it. Once you've earned their trust, you must continue to contribute by delivering on the promises you've made—whether that's putting on a great concert or serving a hot cup of coffee. When you do the right thing, strategically and consistently, the universe will reward you endlessly.

Sharing your energy without intention, without wanting something in return, is one of the most powerful actions any individual or organization can make. It transforms you from a consumer of energy, a taker, to a creator of energy, a giver. This simple act of unselfishly revealing your gifts to the world, adding something to the human experience, contributing, completes the positive energy loop that enables you to unlock your creative potential.

Sharing vs. Advertising

Sharing puts the audience first, while advertising or marketing in the classic sense of the word is selfish—it puts the needs of the individual or organization first. To be a great creator, to share yourself or your ideas effectively, you must share them without selfish intentions; you must put the audience first. Consider the current retail conundrum. For years, stores had seasonal mega-sales. Instead of improving their product, building bonds with their customers, and creating value, they chose to manipulate customers into action with discounts.

The result?

THE MORE GIVING
YOU ARE, THE
MORE LIKELY A
COMMUNITY WILL
EMBRACE YOUR
MESSAGE AND
AMPLIFY IT.

Customers only shop when there are massive sales, profits are eroded, loyalty becomes nonexistent, and, eventually, businesses close. While this applies to the many, a select few have discovered the antidote to this apathy.

In a world where most consumers value meaning over money, experiences over material goods, and crave meaningful connections, the only way to break through is to share, not sell; to be selfless, not selfish.

The components of an effective sharing toolkit—our package of marketing tactics—have changed. For instance, traditional public relations efforts have lost significant influence over consumer behavior with the introduction of social media. As we explained, what used to be a controlled, one-way message, like a restaurant review or gossip column placement, has turned into an active dialogue between brand and consumer: your Instagram or LinkedIn feed. And that dialogue happens primarily through the three critical elements of modern marketing—creative, distribution, and experiential—and you'll need to master them to effectively share your ideas.

Creative

"Creative" (as a noun) encompasses everything from your logo to your social media photos to all the content you produce—videos, photos, blog posts, email newsletters, printed flyers, business cards—and even the way in which you communicate your message. Creative is expressed through content, which is directed toward specific audiences via any form of media, from television to the Internet, smartphones, books, e-books, magazines, and live events. Creative is the product of transforming your idea into sharable forms of messaging people can interact with, relate to, and use, whether on Netflix, Instagram, Spotify, iTunes, YouTube, or any of the other modern platforms.

What does this mean for you?

Consumers, especially those under the age of forty, don't pay attention when they're being sold to directly, especially when the source isn't a trusted one, so your only way in is to entertain and creatively engage them. Your brand must be a wellspring of inspiring, beneficial, and interesting content that reinforces your core value propositions and beliefs—and once you have that, you have to amplify your creative and get it in front of the right eyes.

This brings us to distribution.

Distribution

Sharing is good, and with digital technology, sharing is easy.
—Richard Stallman, Internet activist

Distribution refers to how you share your creative with the consumer. How do you get the word out? Think of your creative as a tree falling in the woods. You can have the best content ever made, but if you can't get eyeballs on it, no one will ever know. In the modern world, digital is the primary way for you to get that message to the most people at the least expense. It is highly efficient, requires minimal investment, and provides instant feedback.

For instance, seventeen percent of the world's population is on Facebook, with many people using the site every day. They provide gobs of information, from where they are hanging out to what they are watching to what they are planning to do and who they are planning to do it with. This is a marketer's bonanza, a strategic sharer's ultimate playground. Google search is similar: if you are signed into your Gmail account when you are searching and using Google Chrome as your browser, then Google basically has access to everything you are doing on the web.

While from a user standpoint this is less than desirable, it provides amazing information to marketers, and for you, that is an enormous opportunity. Digital channels are by far the most effective, efficient, and measurable way to disseminate your idea. The challenge in digital is matching the right message (your "creative") with the right customer, demographic or psychographic. While there are some amazing tools available to help you do that, like Facebook Business Manager and Google Analytics, it really is a high-tech game of trial and error. Test, test, and test again until you find your audience.

The kinds of distribution channels you'll be using generally fall into four buckets:

PAID

Distribution you purchase on any channel, such as Facebook advertisements, Google search advertisements, or just plain old magazine ads or billboards.

OWNED

Distribution points you are in full control of, such as your website(s) or in-room advertisements at a hotel.

SHARED

Your social media channels, where you're part of a community and can actively share your content with that community.

EARNED

This mainly refers to other people talking about you because they like what you're doing. If someone writes an article about your new handbags in *Vogue* or blogs about you, that's earned media, public relations, and referrals.

All these channels work together to reinforce your message. Think of your messaging like items on a menu at a restaurant. Certain items will be sure sellers, such as hamburgers and pizza, while others won't sell, like tripe or snails. You need to determine which of your messages—a/k/a your menu items—are the sure sellers, and which are the dogs. You'll know this through both anecdotal feedback and hard data from your analytics platforms and website usage. Tools like Google Analytics and Facebook Ad Manager are free and easy to use, so you have no excuse not to know more about how your messages are performing. Once you have the information, even if it's just a hunch, you need to combine your messages in a way to yield the best results. Once again, think of this like a menu—you're trying to figure out the combination of appetizer, entrée, and dessert most people will order. Your goal is to filter and refine the feedback so you can focus your resources on the most effective channels and messages. The greater your distribution, the more amplified your message.

Experiential

The third element of modern marketing is experiential. Experiential is where your idea comes to life in some physical form your audience can interact with. This can be in the form of an event, a live marketing activation, or a retail store. Even if your business has no brick-and-mortar presence, it's still very important that customers be able to experience who you are and what you do. That may mean hearing you speak, tasting or sampling your product, or visiting a pop-up. Whatever you choose, the physical manifestation of an idea helps people understand what you do and gives them permission to believe more deeply.

Religion is the best example of this phenomenon in practice. All great religions have places of worship—temples where you can go pray to the god you believe in. These places of worship give individuals a place to gather and reinforce their shared beliefs. It is much easier to be a believer when surrounded by other believers, especially when it is in an environment designed to reinforce those beliefs. Viewed from this perspective, there is no difference between a church, a synagogue, or an Apple store: all three are designed to reinforce beliefs and get people more deeply engaged. It's nearly impossible to create a movement without bringing people together for a shared experience—just imagine how little you would care about your favorite sports team if you couldn't see them play.

The Winning Hand

Back in the marketing dark ages before Google and Facebook, the winning hand for those promoting a product or service was to throw the most resources possible—generally speaking, money spent on advertisements and creative talent for storytelling—at business problems, launches, repositions, etc. And then back up that onslaught with some level of hand-to-hand combat: events and other direct-marketing techniques, like mailing out brochures. That was your advertising campaign.

Was it working?

The only way to know was if the numbers went up or the phones were ringing more than usual.

Today, we don't have that problem. Today, there's a very clear winning hand—a surefire way to reach your audience, to demonstrate the value of your marketing efforts. And this winning hand is enabled by, though not limited to, digital.

Let me expand on this.

In the short term, you need cover. In the business world, cover comes with revenue and cash flow. The best way for marketers to show return on investment is to focus their spend on low-funnel, measurable, high-return channels. Digital marketing is that channel, and within it, Google is the lowest part of the funnel, used by prospective customers who already intend to do something. Digital is the salvation of the marketer. No longer should marketers be dragged over the coals by their peers or bosses for spending money with no measurable return. Now, marketers can show exactly how many clicks, purchases, views, and other engagements their efforts receive to demonstrate the ROI—return on investment—of their marketing spend. Digital is the short-term cover we always dreamed of, and it's part one of the winning hand.

Short-term revenue is great and necessary, especially in a society obsessed with *now*. But there's far greater value that can be generated by creating a trusted brand. Think of it this way: You may buy something today because it's on sale, but that doesn't mean you'll buy it again later. The brands you love—the ones you're loyal to—you'll continue to consume for many years into the future whether they're on sale or not. That's long-term brand value, and that results in far greater revenue over time than the short-term income generated from picking up the low-hanging fruit on digital. Therefore, the second part of the winning hand is brand-building. While this can and should be done partly through digital awareness channels like Instagram or an owned content platform like a blog or newsletter, the practice of branding is done through a consistent aspirational dialogue with your audience. Build trust, put their needs ahead of your own, inspire them and improve their lives, and combine that with a strong perceived value, and you'll have a customer for life. But that doesn't happen overnight; that requires consistent investment without a clear short-term return.

To achieve marketing success, you must have both revenue and relevance. That can only be achieved by effectively implementing both parts of a winning hand, the magic and the math. Satisfy the skeptics with the only thing that cannot be debated, short-term revenue and ROI, and then invest the time to build the thing that everyone really desires: long-term brand value and loyalty. That is the winning hand in the Age of Ideas.

Direct Influence

When I was first appointed chief marketing officer of a hotel company, I was presented with an interesting situation, one I'm quite sure many marketing professionals have experienced in some form over the last five to ten years.

It was Fashion Week in New York City, and we'd allotted a small budget to offer complimentary rooms to some social influencers. It was 2014, and this type of marketing wasn't as common as it is today, so we didn't pay any fees, and the lost potential revenue for the hotel was minimal—maybe ten thousand dollars max. The influencers were engaged through the relationships of our head of social media. We invited fifteen, ten accepted, and they stayed for two or three days each in exchange for multiple daily posts showcasing the property.

During the same week, another one of our hotels was featured on the *Condé Nast Traveler* Gold List as one of the best hotels in the world. For years, this list was paramount when it came to attracting high-end guests willing to pay a premium for your property.

The entire executive team of the company was ecstatic at the hotel's inclusion on the Condé Nast list. High fives! Congratulations all around! Meanwhile, no one made a single positive comment about the ten influencers we were able to get, at a minimal expense, to stay at our hotel. We'd spent more than one hundred thousand dollars on public relations agencies to be included on that Condé Nast list and less than 10 percent of that cost to acquire those influencers. Now, at the time, *Condé Nast Traveler* had no more than 300,000 followers on their Instagram feed and a rapidly diminishing print circulation, while the ten influencers had well over 10-million-and-growing engaged followers on their social media platforms. One of them was Aimee Song (@songofstyle), who boasts 4.9 million followers on just her Instagram platform alone. And these influencers didn't just post once, they posted multiple times daily on their channels. Though we didn't at the time have the digital analytics to measure the full effect—traffic and bookings—of both channels, I believe the return on investment from the influencer posts was significantly higher, considering the cost, number of followers, engagement levels, clickthroughs, and reposts.

This experience is a prime example of how marketing has changed in the Age of Ideas.

Influence isn't a new concept born from influencers; all advertising and marketing has always been based on influence—it's why we used to buy full-page magazine ads, TV commercials, and vie for the attention of magazine editors. But with the democratization of communication and technology, there has been a shift in who has the influence, a fragmenting of influence, and without a doubt this will continue to evolve. While some influencers are highly valuable, some are not. While some magazines and newspapers are highly influential, some are not. As marketers and entrepreneurs, we need to move away from relying on any one outlet or person who at the moment may have the power and instead build our own influence, like Supreme does. You can do that by establishing a strong direct relationship with your audience.

In an ever-changing landscape, the best way to build influence is through a direct relationship on platforms you own, like a website or email newsletter. Secondary platforms like social media, Amazon, or YouTube are amazingly impactful as well, especially for building awareness and finding new customers, but you are at the whim of the company running the platform. The more direct a relationship you have, the more you control your influence, and the less dependent you are on middle-men that will eventually cost you money and dilute your message. Remember, a platform is there to generate profits and please all users, not just serve you and your needs. Shareholders will eventually force publicly traded platforms to monetize.

In the Age of Ideas, influence equals freedom. The more you have, the more opportunities you have to create value for yourself, your partners, and your audience. This thought must be paramount in every interaction you have with your followers—if they trust you and engage with you, then your influence is growing. Influence is critical to your success in the modern paradigm, no matter your pursuit.

Collaboration

As we continue to develop this concept of strategic sharing, it's important to look at another avenue that carries rich possibilities in the Age of Ideas: collaboration.

Collaboration is another vital marketing tool enabling participants to effectively share their message with an engaged audience at scale. Collaborators exchange trust, energy, and credibility, and ideally enhance each other's relative influence. When one brand agrees to collaborate with another, they're telling their audience, "I dig what this brand does, and you should, too." Collaboration is word-of-mouth on a massive scale.

For instance, H&M is known for their capsule collaborations with high-end fashion designers like Alexander Wang and Balmain. There's no other channel I know of that could have authentically increased Alexander Wang's following with an engaged audience better than H&M. H&M got relevance and financial returns, and Wang got financial returns and aspirational exposure to his future customer base.

Mutual Admiration + Creative Execution = Shared Audience Growth

When it comes to collaborations, each contributor needs to get something they want. Supreme's collaboration with Louis Vuitton—one of the largest and most well-respected fashion brands in the world—is a great example.

While their collaboration was a big deal in the fashion world, the amount of product sold represents a very small portion of Louis Vuitton's and probably even Supreme's gross revenues. This exchange had more to do with relevance, exposure, and long-term brand value. For Supreme, a street-style brand, collaborating with Louis Vuitton was a crowning achievement. It was the ultimate seal of approval for their brand equity and strategic vision—the exposure to millions of new, vetted customers was just a bonus. For Louis Vuitton, collaborating with one of the most relevant street-style brands in the world reinforced their continued relevance and gave them a foothold with a new breed of influencer. While the collaboration sold out (and currently resells for 10x original retail), both brands received increased engagement, exposure, and influence. That's the power of collaboration.

Storytelling

Right now, you are a legend in your own mind. Though you can see your idea in your head or even in your hand, the greater universe is not yet aware of what you have to offer. Through strategic sharing your audience will awaken to who you are and what you have created or intend to create. The goal is for you, your ideas, and your creations to become legendary in everyone else's mind. Let me explain.

A legend is a compelling, especially well-known individual, group, or narrative. Legends are often associated with an exceptional skill, capability, or event. Take, for example, the story of how Steve Jobs and Steve Wozniak founded Apple. This origin story ends with the creation of the most valuable company in human history and made Jobs, Wozniak, and their brand legendary. What started simply as an idea eventually transformed all involved into legends through great storytelling. It is no different than the story of how Obama became president, the story of the founding of our country,

Mutual Admiration

+

Creative Execution

=

Shared Audience Growth

or the story of the parting of the Dead Sea. These stories transformed the people, ideas, and things involved into legends. Storytelling is the most effective form of communication we have, and learning to do it well is a critical tool in your strategic sharing toolbox.

The story you tell about the origin and development of your idea will play a big role in whether or not your audience engages. For example, I am sure there were countless behind-the-scenes deals, power struggles, and petty moments that went into Barack Obama becoming our first African-American president. But the story told is of his heroic rise from obscurity to barrier-breaking world leader. Or, going back further, without a doubt there were extreme amounts of death, destruction, and massive shifts of wealth and power that went into the formation of America, but the story we're told conjures an upstart nation fueled by democratic ideals overthrowing an exploitative empire.

The stories we like to hear are ones that make us feel good, that are entertaining, exciting, inspirational, and easy to remember. With this in mind, as you craft your origin story, you should consider the following:

1. **Simplicity & Positivity:** Keep your story and messaging simple, direct, and positive. You have mere seconds to grab a customer's attention, so make your message clear. And keep your messages upbeat, focusing on the *solving* aspect of your creation's problem-solution equation. As for negativity, no one wants to hear someone complain.

2. **Repeatable:** Give your customers something they can easily share with their friends and that they *want* to share with their friends. A bar in New York recently made a spicy chicken wing covered in hot sauce made with liquid gold. While this is clearly ridiculous, it is also very easily repeatable. *Did you see those hot wings made with gold?* Insert opinion, share video. A short, impactful story is easiest for us to remember and repeat.

3. **Relatable or Aspirational:** Can you see yourself doing the same thing as the people in the story? Do you want to see

yourself doing the same thing as the people in the story? If you want to engage a particular audience, make sure they are able to connect with your story or maybe even aspire to be part of your story. The audience should hear your story and say, "Yes, I agree," or "I have felt like that too," or "I want to do that," or "be that way."

4. **Struggle:** Nobody is perfect, and knowing that everyone experiences struggle is a notably comforting feeling for someone who is struggling. Beyond that, it's appealing to root for the underdog, a position most of us have experienced. When you tell your story, remember that people want to know something about a challenge or struggle you have encountered or are encountering on your journey to success. Since living a fulfilled life and manifesting astonishing success invariably requires overcoming a struggle, it shouldn't be too hard to find your own stories of struggle that people can relate to.

5. **Redemption:** All struggle ends with some form of redemption for the hero. Give your story a happy ending. If that's hard to do because you're still struggling, then point to the light at the end of the tunnel—illuminate the knowledge you have gained and the challenge you are on your way to overcoming. This will provide a payoff to your audience and allow them to further invest in your successes.

Humans crave stories—it's how we share and connect with one another. We constantly tell and share these stories, so getting yours to be part of the conversation is important to the sharing and amplification of your idea. For that to happen your story must be told and reinforced on all of your channels, both owned and paid. The more your story is repeated, refined, and accepted by your tribe, the more a groundswell of support will grow for you and your pursuits. This support will eventually form a community, or as some call it, a tribe. The more your story is told, the closer you will be to becoming a legend...and as they say, legends never die.

A24

Moonlight.
Ladybird.
The Disaster Artist.
A Most Violent Year.
It Comes at Night.
Spring Breakers.
The Lobster.
The Florida Project.
Amy.
Supersonic
Ex Machina.

Almost every movie that has meant something to me over the past five-plus years has been made by A24, an independent film company started in 2012 in New York. When I see their logo (an awesome one, by the way), I anticipate I'll be taken on a journey of emotional discovery, experiencing a life or points of view that provoke deep thought and consideration.

Early on, while admiring their logo and loving their films, I didn't know much about A24 and how they became such prolific enablers of great creative work. But in writing this book, I began researching the company, watching it more closely, and marveled repeatedly at the way A24 has proved exceptional at strategic sharing. Not only do does this studio foster superlative films, it demonstrates a profound understanding of how digital media, storytelling, collaboration, direct influence, and trust-building can propel a company from zero to sixty in the Age of Ideas.

Like Supreme, David Chang, or Ian Schrager, A24 makes a product that intrigues me, that inspires excitement, aspiration, and irrational loyalty. What do I mean by irrational loyalty? I mean the willingness to pay more for a branded product or service with minimal added practical benefit. I listen to the A24 podcast and I'm signed up to the A24 email list. I follow their social media feeds. This isn't the way I usually engage with movie companies. A24 has developed a direct-to-consumer relationship with me and become my trusted film curator. When their latest release comes out, I don't even need to check reviews because I believe in them and the work they're doing. They've consistently delivered great films, and this has led me to trust them with my entertainment needs.

And now I know their origin story.

In 2012, Daniel Katz, David Fenkel, and John Hodges left their jobs at Guggenheim Partners, Oscilloscope, and Big Beach, respectively, to start a new, independent film company aimed at redefining the way indie movies were made and marketed. As Katz explained, "I always had dreams of [starting a company]. And on some level, honestly, I was afraid to go out on my own and try to make it work. And I was with a bunch of friends [driving] into Rome and I kind of had this moment of clarity. And it was on the A24 [motorway]. And in that moment I was like: *Now it's time to go do this*."

Katz and his fellow founders had been great admirers of 1990s independent cinema and felt there was now a void when it came to films with that kind of boldness and artistic quality. They decided to start a New York-based company focused on "the films and filmmakers, not us." This meant they would give the creatives—the directors and the writers—control of their work. As Harmony Korine, director of *Spring Breakers*, puts it, "Hollywood is run by accountants at this point. And so anytime you speak with someone who's not a pure accountant, is not a pencil pusher, it's exciting. They had heart to them."

And that heart has made all the difference with filmmakers. While this approach is not new or novel, it's rare. Entrepreneurs and business leaders who are open-minded and intelligent enough to enable creatives while providing them support and expertise to realize a truly differentiated vision are few and far between, but the ones who do it well are able to leave their mark on culture and exponentially improve their returns.

Viewed through the lens of our Age of Ideas thesis, A24 represents a prime example of the Creator's Formula in action. The

IRRATIONAL
LOYALTY:
THE WILLINGNESS
TO PAY MORE
FOR A BRANDED
PRODUCT OR
SERVICE WITH
MINIMAL ADDED
PRACTICAL
BENEFIT.

studio enables gifted filmmakers—experienced creatives—to tell distinct, emotionally generous stories from a personal perspective. And it has developed marketing expertise and credibility after repeated, flawless execution. The way A24 supports its filmmakers' creative expression while also doing everything right when it comes to the strategic sharing of its movies with the world has created a brand that has few peers in the world of entertainment.

Four years after its inception, the company's first original production, *Moonlight*, won the Academy Award for Best Picture. As of 2018, A24 has received a total of twenty-four Academy Award nominations, including a Best Picture nomination for *Lady Bird*, plus a Golden Globe nomination (Best Motion Picture–Musical or Comedy) for *The Disaster Artist*.

A24's marketing is innovative, even brilliant. Out of necessity early on, they turned to lower-cost digital platforms and creative guerrilla marketing tactics to build buzz around their films. And while these tactics cost less, such platforms, as we've been exploring, are also notably effective in the modern market, especially with the under-forty demographic.

Their film *Ex Machina* premiered at the 2015 SXSW Festival, and A24 used the dating app Tinder to market to unwitting festival visitors. When Tinder users clicked on an attractive woman named Ava, she would engage and eventually invite them to check out her Instagram. When potential daters visited her Insta page, it featured only a trailer for *Ex Machina*. This was not only an incredibly creative and engaging marketing tactic to target socially active festivalgoers, it reinforced the film's premise of artificial intelligence and in itself was buzzworthy. The film ended up being received very positively at the festival and went on to become a hit at the box office, grossing $35 million on a $15-million production budget.

Lady Bird has been A24's greatest financial success to date, grossing over $75 million on a $10-million production budget, and the company has recently expanded into the growing television-content business. While A24 has had its share of financial misses as well, it has succeeded beyond compare at building a deep connection to filmgoers and consumers of entertainment programming. And it's done this by establishing a direct relationship with its audience and telling meaningful, beautiful stories.

Let me say a bit more about this relationship to audiences. Imagine if Steven Spielberg had a personal email list and multiple social media channels personally connecting him with all the filmgoers who have seen his movies during the last forty or so years. While Spielberg does have an immense brand, the main way he communicates with his audience is through mass media and expensive, metric-resistant platforms such as billboards and television commercials. By contrast, A24 has a direct relationship with a young, active audience and personal relationships with filmmakers who themselves enjoy close connections to their audiences. Both A24 and their collaborators can reach their audience directly at little or no cost to the parent company and the project they're promoting. These one- or two-degree separations between brand and consumer give A24 reliable and growing influence in the entertainment industry. The studio not only has created an ideal platform for genuine creative storytellers, they have a machine in place to directly share with their customers and the expertise to collaboratively amplify their messages.

But none of this would have been possible without them first building trust, and that can only happen when you repeatedly and consistently deliver on your promises.

Repetition & Consistency

My close friend Josh Shames has a distinct expertise in turning annoying inside-jokes into timeless classics. He starts by coming up with a joke or saying something he thinks is amusing, such as shouting "herry ep" after every single request he makes. For example, he'll say, "Can you get me some iced tea and throw a bit of hurry ep sauce on it." When he first says it, you think he's annoying, rude, and slightly off-kilter. But then he keeps saying it, over and over and over again, and it grows on you. By the thirtieth time, it starts becoming part of your lingo. All of a sudden, you're accidentally using his joke, telling your mom to "hurry ep" with dinner. By the fiftieth time, you've made it your own, you begin to find joy in repeating it, and you can't stop. It's his particular brand of humor, and his consistency and repetition make you eventually love it, too.

When it comes to the sharing strategies we've been discussing, repetition and consistency are crucial to using them effectively.

Repetition is the performing of an action over and over again. Messages can only break through to our deeper consciousness when they're repeated. As Schopenhauer said, "All truth passes through three stages. First, it is ridiculed. Second, it is violently opposed. Third, it is accepted as being self-evident." The only way to get past ridicule and violent opposition is to practice repetition.

Consistency is when the quality of a product or service doesn't vary greatly over time. Every great brand is consistent. We've just seen how potent consistency can be when we examined the story of A24. It's this independent studio's ability to deliver one moving, artfully made film after another that has won my deep loyalty, turning me into a "true fan." The practice of brand management is actually defined as managing what makes you consistently different. Name any product you think of as great and you'll realize the consistent delivery of quality is what makes the product that way. Coca-Cola? Google? Mercedes? The reason people use their products is because they've consistently met or exceeded their promise over time. If your Coca-Cola didn't consistently taste the way you expected it to, or Google didn't consistently provide the search results you were looking for, you'd find another product that did.

Brands, products, and people can only manifest their full potential when they're able to combine repetition with consistency. To unlock your potential you must show up every day and reinforce what you want the world to know about you. Just like my old friend Josh Shames or your local pop radio station, you must repeat your message consistently until your audience begins to embrace what makes you different.

Trust

Josh is also a great friend, the kind you can count on no matter what. And he's this way not only with me, but with a large group of people he has known since he was very young. He is a trusted friend because he puts the needs of others ahead of his own. Being a trusted friend is his defining characteristic. Your goal is to be a trusted brand and that results from practicing strategic, generous sharing. Trust is, as we've noted, the most important connection you need to establish with your community.

ALL TRUTH
PASSES THROUGH
THREE STAGES.
FIRST, IT IS RIDICULED.
SECOND, IT IS
VIOLENTLY OPPOSED.
THIRD, IT IS
ACCEPTED AS BEING
SELF-EVIDENT.

We're constantly taking in information and categorizing it based on our level of trust for the source. As an example, let's look at New York newspapers. The king of NYC papers is the *New York Times*. The *Times* has been reporting the news for more than 150 years and is widely considered the pinnacle of reliable news outlets. The *Times* will only print stories if there are multiple reputable sources. For the *Times*, getting it right is more important than getting it first. On the opposite end of the spectrum is the *New York Post*. The cover of the *Post* is regularly strewn with over-the-top headlines and it's filled with sensational tabloid stories. It's famous for its gossip column, and the content is more entertainment than education.

The *New York Times* is the friend you reach out to for serious advice—more trust; the *New York Post* is the friend you have fun with—less trust.

The continuum of trust is directly related to value. When trust for a brand is high, we're willing to pay more or make purchases with less consideration. For instance, Mercedes starts convincing you of the superiority of their automobiles when you're young. The intention is to build your trust in the brand so one day, when you have the means, you'll purchase a Mercedes. It's crazy to think, but the sales cycle of a Mercedes actually starts thirty or forty years before you make a purchase; we buy promises, not products. When trust exists, you don't have to manipulate customer behavior with discounts or sales, you only have to effectively and consistently communicate your story. Trust is a long-term play.

The same theory applies to individuals. Your name and reputation make up your brand. Your coworkers, friends, and even family value you similarly to the way you value a product. While this may sound clinical, it's true. Let's just consider the arena of employment. We're more likely to hire someone and pay that person a higher salary if we trust her. I would even venture to say that when investing in someone's business idea, how much we trust her is more important than whether we believe in the idea.

Being considered trustworthy may be the single most important factor toward achieving your goals in the new paradigm. Ironically, though, how we evaluate trustworthiness has barely changed since the beginning of time. We make these decisions almost entirely based on our instincts and emotions. What do they look like? What do they sound like? What is their reputation? Therefore, all of the sharing strategies we talked about, from Storytelling to Collaboration to Repetition, are fundamentally about building trust. You must understand your audience and then package your message in a way that makes your audience feel an emotional connection.

Once you've won the trust of your audience, protect it, because if that bond is broken, it's nearly impossible to fix.

CONCLUSION

The End & Your New Beginning

Success, like happiness, cannot be pursued; it must ensue, and it only does so as the unintended side-effect of one's personal dedication to a cause greater than oneself or as the by-product of one's surrender to a person other than oneself. Happiness must happen, and the same holds for success: you have to let it happen by not caring about it.

—Viktor Frankl

We have more freedom than at any time in human history.

But the majority of us do nothing with this freedom.

Instead, we impose constraints on ourselves, despite fighting so hard to remove these constraints.

We decide what's possible and enforce artificial limits on our lives.

We do this because it makes us comfortable; it feels manageable, it's just easier.

But as Abraham Maslow explained, the pinnacle of life is the enjoyment of "peak experiences."

Today, these "rare, exciting, oceanic, deeply moving, exhilarating, elevating experiences" are within your grasp.

All you have to do is be open and available to where the universe wants to take you.

Put away your fears and go.

After all, you're free.

But what do you do when you have infinite possibilities?

How do you proceed?

The primary goal of freedom is a fulfilled existence.

And while it's exciting to have an endless variety of hot dogs, work-out programs, and luxury automobiles, these material elements of life have little or no bearing on your true happiness and fulfillment.

Our powers lie within.

The mysteries of life, the true might of the human experience, exist in life's emotional aspects. How do we feel about who we are? How do we feel about our loved ones? What do we create and share? How do we make others feel? Our emotional worldview determines what we're able to manifest and, most importantly, how we feel about our life experience. Therefore, the understanding of your emotions and the emotions of the people with whom you surround yourself is paramount to a meaningful life.

While we all desire happiness and fulfillment, popular culture gives us all the wrong directions on how to reach these goals. The fulfillment we all seek only comes from being creative in our daily life and sharing that creativity with others. This doesn't mean you need to be a painter and live the life of an artist. It means acting on your creative impulses, pursuing your purpose, whether as an accountant, entrepreneur, or guitarist, engaging in a skill you find challenging and enjoyable.

The result of this approach will be your best work.

From here, your success and fulfillment will ensue.

The Age of Ideas has arrived.

Today, applying your creativity will not only bring you fulfillment, it is the primary skill you need to create value.

It's time for you to be truly free.

It's time to spend your brief time on earth doing the things you love, surrounded by the people you care about the most.

It's time to share what makes you special and serve the needs of others through a purpose greater than your selfish desires.

Now is the time to realize the gift you've been given.

Today is when you make it happen.

Do it for all of us. We can't wait to see the magic you make.

APPENDIX

Tools of Magic

Act always as if the future of the universe depended on what you did, while laughing at yourself for thinking that whatever you do makes any difference.

—Buddhist proverb

Knowledge is power. But without practice it is impossible to transform and manifest that power for the benefit of yourself and others. Over the years I have developed some simple practices that I feel have greatly benefited my well-being and ability to manifest my truth.

You are the most creative and destructive force in your life. Therefore controlling your "monkey mind"—our tendency to amplify and indulge unhelpful inclinations—is one of the most important steps you can take in neutralizing your negative habits and empowering your positive self. Below you will find a selection of tools I utilize to help me get through the day in the best possible way. And remember, all of these techniques are compounding—meaning the more you do them, the more effective they become.

Meditation

Our minds were not built for the barrage of stimulation we experience in today's world. The only way to ensure we do not overload it is to put in place practices like meditation and exercise to relieve the pressure and stress we are under. Meditation is the lowest-cost approach, in terms of time and effort, and yields the highest benefit, in terms of well-being, that you can invest in. I cannot recommend it highly enough.

Our breath has incredible power over our mind and body. In a world filled with anxieties about the past and the future, it's hard to be in the now. Meditation—the act of using your breath and focusing on one specific thing to calm your mind—brings you into the present. While many people use meditation without the additional tools below, for me it works best in concert with these other practices.

I have practiced guided meditation both in person and through apps or taped tracks, and mantra meditation through the practice of Transcendental Meditation. Both work well for me. Meditation offers substantial physical health and fulfillment benefits. A regular practice of 10-30 minutes a day will noticeably enhance your existence.

Intense Exercise

As a young man I was physically fit. I was very involved in sports and took up weightlifting toward the end of high school and early in college. Then I went to Italy for a year abroad and everything went haywire. Eating and drinking—indulging as often as possible—took over for the gym. My exercise routine from the latter part of college into my mid-thirties consisted of low-intensity gym workouts, with maybe 20 minutes on the treadmill and some light weightlifting. I thought I was working out, but the truth is I was just sweating enough to make myself feel okay before I indulged again.

Fitness-wise, I was losing the battle with Father Time.

Over the years I began to feel worse, with diminished energy. And I didn't feel as good about myself. Eventually it began to negatively impact my relationship with my family and that was when I said enough. I attended a high-energy group fitness class with my friends Jack and Josh, taught by the legendary athletes Laird Hamilton, a big-wave surfer, and Gabby Reece, an Olympic volleyball player.

This class was amazing not only because I got a great workout, but because I felt like I was in it with the rest of the group. We were supporting one another. From there I tried Barry's Bootcamp and I have been hooked ever since. The combination of dynamic music and being part of a community is addictive. And the intensity of the exercise is far greater then I would have ever gotten with a trainer, from yoga, or from any other workout I have encountered. By no means am I saying Barry's Bootcamp is the answer for everyone, but high-intensity workouts like Barry's, Cross Fit, and SoulCycle have a reliably positive impact on us being able to manifest our dreams. The intense exercise, esprit-de-corps, and inspiring support-mechanisms help you be your best self.

Monkey-Mind Morning Pages

As mentioned above, our monkey mind can get us into all types of trouble. It makes us see, feel, and react to things that aren't really happening. The best way I have found to neutralize the monkey mind is to let all the thoughts running around in my head escape first thing every morning. What I do is to pick up the NotePad on my iPhone or a basic paper notepad and just write out my stream of consciousness. I write everything I am thinking and feeling the minute I wake up. The monkey-mind state usually lasts for about 5-10 minutes and definitely diminishes in time the more days in a row I do the writing. By getting rid of all the garbage in my head in some formalized manner, the unhelpful consciousness just goes away. I am then free to apply my mind to productive, positive things that are worthy of my brain's energy.

Your First-Principle Truths

You're constantly changing, and so is your environment. By nature, your highest and best challenge will be changing, too. A simple example from my life would be the birth of my two sons, a year and a half apart. From that time forward, my priorities shifted and my environment changed—which inevitably transformed my ideal pursuit. For your own growth and fulfillment, it's important you recognize, accept, and evolve with these changes as they happen.

But some things don't change, they don't evolve. These are first principles: fundamental concepts—laws of nature, humanity, and life—that hold true for every stage of our journeys.

For me, there are so many thoughts flowing through my mind every day that I find it hard to remember my first-principle truths without some method of reinforcement.

The north-star intentions I want to guide my behavior and decision-making become clouded in the onslaught of information. Consequently, I find it valuable to write down my first-principle truths every morning after I do my monkey-mind morning pages. The idea is this: First, clean out your mind with the pages, and then fill it up with the good stuff—your most bedrock values. Taking the time to list these anchoring precepts reminds you of what you value and how you would like to act on a regular basis.

Here's one of my intention lists to help you form one of your own.

1. Be a channel of positivity in the world.
2. Help those less fortunate—remove pain.
3. Connect deeply with my wife, kids, and family on a regular basis.
4. Be in harmony with the surrounding energy.
5. Let nothing sway my equilibrium.
6. Do what I need to be strong. Protect my body and mind.
7. Pursue large and worthy challenges.
8. Earn enough to provide a beautiful life for my family.
9. Be in the moment, and be proud of who I am without any external approvals or qualifiers.
10. Be gray, not black and white.
11. Exemplify patience and faith.
12. Accept challenges as gifts.
13. Encourage and assist my wife.
14. Embrace fear, and dance with it patiently.
15. Let my ego go—kill it.
16. Never compare; it is the root of all evil.
17. Remember what I value.
18. Focus. Do one thing really well.
19. Appreciate my blessings.
20. Let my journey ensue.

THANK YOU

Alan Philips is a creative executive, entrepreneur, writer, & speaker specializing in guiding and inspiring individuals and organizations on the path to discovering their purpose & unlocking their creative potential. Alan has over two decades of experience in hospitality, real estate, and entrepreneurship working with some of the world's most recognized organizations, people, and brands. For more information on The Age of Ideas and Alan Philips or to sign up for our weekly newsletter, visit theageofideas.com or email alan@theageofideas.com.

NOTES, QUOTES, & IDEAS

THE AGE OF IDEAS

NOTES, QUOTES, & IDEAS